All about the Lurcher

Frontispiece A jumble of lurchers waiting to enter the show ring at Lambourn: an example of the placid temperament of well-trained individual dogs at a crowded event.

All about the Lurcher

KATHARINE TOTTENHAM

PELHAM BOOKS

First published in Great Britain by
Pelham Books Ltd
27 Wrights Lane,
London W8 5TZ
1983
Reprinted 1985, 1987
© 1983 by Katharine Tottenham

British Library Cataloguing in Publication Data

Tottenham, Katharine
    All about the Lurcher
    1. Lurcher
    I. Title
    636.7'53   SF429.L87

ISBN 0 7207 1441 9

Phototypeset by *Sunrise Setting*, Torquay,
and printed and bound by
Butler & Tanner Ltd, Frome

Contents

Illustrations

Acknowledgements

The author would like to thank the following people and organisations for their help in supplying photographs for this book:

John Kimber 1–15, 17–27, 29–32; Sunday Times *Frontispiece*, 36, 38–39; Stanley Hurwitz 33–35, 37; North Creake Photography 40,41.

Introduction

One eighteenth century writer defines lurchers as the constant companions of poachers '... of the most unprincipled and abandoned description'. It is only in recent years that it has gained respectability as a sporting dog and, in common with Jack Russell terriers, has now become popular because of its attractive appearance and, usually, high IQ. Nevertheless, the prospective owner of a lurcher should understand the origins and characteristics of the 'breed' before buying a puppy which may grow up to become a dog that is totally unsuited to the family's way of life.

This sad state of affairs happens all too often with pedigree working breeds such as labradors, border collies and alsatians when they are expected to live as idle pets while their instincts urge them to hunt or herd: such dogs are liable to become neurotic or to expend pent-up energy on the excitement of worrying farm livestock. Therefore, it is important to realise that a lurcher is part greyhound and, as such, needs a great deal of exercise once it is full grown, and that other breeds in its ancestry have been bred-in to add intelligence and the ability and willingness to be trained for a specific form of sport.

A good lurcher is strictly obedient; a keen, silent worker able to use all its innate cleverness to course game, make a quick kill and retrieve to hand. However, most will settle happily in the role of companion – lying by the fire, travelling by car and accompanying its owner out shopping or to the pub – but it must be trained to be obedient, given an interest in life and plenty of exercise which ought to include an opportunity to work now and again. In this situation a lurcher can be one of the most charming and devoted of all sporting dogs.

1 History of Long-dogs in England

THE origin of the lurcher is bound up with the gypsies and with the greyhound, and both date back to prehistory. When scholars began to study the evolution of language in the eighteenth century they found that Sanskrit, the ancient language of India, was the first to be written down in literary form as the four sacred books of Hindu scripture. In more recent times, those interested in the Romany language have found it to be based on Hindi, spoken in the Punjab and other parts of north West India, which has itself evolved from Sanskrit. This places the gypsy as being of Asian rather than Middle Eastern descent, and suggests that these people are related to the nomadic Banjaras of Northern India who use a rough-haired small greyhound of lurcher type to hunt their food.

Blue. A fine example of a typical Norfolk lurcher: a true long-dog with plenty of heart-room and good bone, she has successfully hunted rabbits, hare and small deer for her master's larder, and yet enjoys the comforts of home where she is kind and gentle.

Similarity persists in the fact that the Banjaras are treated with some suspicion by the settled population because they 'live off the country', eating peculiar food including agama lizards (an Asian type of iguana), a small monkey known as the loris, and a creature called a pangolin or spiney anteater which, in common with the European hedgehog, rolls itself up as a means of defence and is baked in this attitude inside a covering of clay.

About a thousand years ago some of these nomadic people began to wander into the Middle East and then on across Europe to arrive in Britain around the fourteenth century, no doubt bringing with them horses and dogs, together with their skills as tinkers working metal and the crafty ability to poach anything edible from the countryside.

Since hunting in medieval times was the prerogative of the king and the nobility, the Forest Laws of England were draconian in the extreme: peasants were allowed to keep dogs small enough to pass through a ring seven inches in diameter and also working sheepdogs (whose main task was as guards against wolves); any other type of dog was crippled either by being ham-strung or by having the toes of a front foot chopped off to render it hopelessly lame. A person caught poaching faced capital punishment. This state of affairs meant that a gypsy and his dog were in constant danger and both learned to go about their business secretly and silently – the dog 'lurking' in cover when strangers were about.

One of the first books written on the subject of field sports in England was *Ye Boke of Huntying* by a lady named Julyana Berners, Prioress of Sopwell, in the late 1400s (although Brian Vesey-Fitzgerald disputes her authorship and transfers it to one Julia Barnes of the same period); but, regardless of who wrote it, its main interest lies in her list of known breeds at that time, which begins, 'First ther is a grehownd ...' and later describes in verse the ideal greyhound and its management:

> A grehoun should be headed like a snake,
> An necked like a drake,
> Footed like a cat,
> Tayled like a rat,
> Syded like a team,
> Chyned[1] like a beam
> Ye first he must learn to feed,
> Ye secon year to field hym lead,
> Ye third year he is fellow-like,[2]
> Ye fourth year there is none sike,[3]
> Ye fifth year he is good enow,
> Ye sixth year he shall hold-ye-plow[4]
> Ye seventh year he will avail
> Great bitches to assail,

Ye eighth year lick ladle,[5]
Ye ninth year cart saddle,[6]
And when he is comen to that year
Have him to the tanner,
For ye best houn that ever bitch had,
At nine year he is full bad.

[1] chyne: backbone
[2] fellow-like: useful
[3] sike: such
[4] hold-ye-plow: be strong
[5] lick ladle: kitchen pet
[6] cart saddle: a warm jacket

It is sad that even her best hounds ended their days at the age of nine in a tanner's yard, where dogs skins were cured to make gloves for ladies and jesses for hawks. She makes no mention of size or coat texture for the simple reason that greyhounds then, and up until the eighteenth century, varied in height from that of a whippet to near-deerhound size and the coat could be either rough or smooth.

Some hundred years earlier two manuscripts on hunting had been written: one, *Le Livre de Chasse*, by the French count Gaston de Foix; the other a treatise on hunting by an Englishman named Guillaume Twici who was huntsman to Edward II. The quarry to which Forest Laws applied listed hare, hart (deer), otter, boar, wolf and fox in descending order of precedence, and the hare was described as 'the king of all venery'; it is, therefore, not surprising that the greyhound was the most popular hunting dog of those times, or that its ownership was prohibited to the common people.

It has been suggested that initial crossbreeding between greyhounds and sheepdogs were attempts at disguise when anyone who was not a nobleman, seen out with a coursing dog could be certain of dying on a gibbet. These half-bred animals were often docked as an added deception – although tails were also cut off in the belief that this prevented rabies. Whatever the reason, gypsies and poachers alike soon discovered the worth of a lurcher which was so much more intelligent than a pure hound. But this was the only link between gypsies and country poeple who looked on these wandering foreigners with suspicion and a certain awe: rumour had it that they were a lost Egyptian tribe headed by former kings and princes and so Romany families became known as Egyptians and then as gypsies. The gypsy is never slow to see an advantage and, clearly, it was useful to acquire royal descent and a reputation for sooth-saying, not to mention the possession of 'the evil eye', which could harm your family or livestock.

Della. Just under 56cm (22in) in height this greyhound/sheepdog cross qualifies for small smooth lurcher classes. She works well in the field and has proved herself as a brood bitch producing rough and smooth puppies.

This fear exists in many places today. I have been warned by several countrywomen never to turn away a gypsy from the doorstep: you must buy their wares or give them money, or at least a cake and a cup of tea, or woe betide you. In fact, I have never received anything but courtesy from these much-maligned people.

The old Forest Laws continued in force until the latter part of the sixteenth century when they were modified in the reign of James I by a statute which permitted owners of land valued at a minimum of £40 a year to keep greyhounds. This was a comparatively large sum, but even so allowed more prosperous yeomen to enjoy the sport of coursing for the first time (at least officially). The law based on land value survived until the early 1800s and so did drastic penalties for poaching: yet every village had its poacher, sometimes driven by hunger but often by the spice of dicing if not with death, then with a chance of deportation to a penal colony.

A group of people who appear to have been more or less immune to the law were drovers. They herded animals destined for meat markets to cities all over the country, and used dogs to drive the cattle and sheep and to hunt game for the pot along the way. The best dog for the purpose was a lurcher bred from a sheepdog and it needed to be both tough and intelligent to survive a life of driving flocks over miles of road all day; scouring woods and fields to find its master's supper when the drove halted at dusk; then catch something for its own food and finally find shelter in a hedge where it could sleep. Few can have lived long, particularly as drovers were a brawling, cruel lot and unlikely to take much account of a dog's welfare, but, despite this, lurchers were being bred to a recognisable type, at least, by the end of the eighteenth century.

While lurchers could be seen in most parts of England in company with gypsies, poachers and drovers, probably the best known was the Norfolk which brought livestock from East Anglia to London's Smithfield meat market: this dog may be considered as the archetypical lurcher, described as '… about three fourths the heights and size of a full grown greyhound, and of a yellowish or sandy red colour, rough and wiry haired, with ears naturally erect, but dropping a little at the point …'. It was generally called a Norfolk lurcher.

Boggy. A rescued stray, this shaggy dog represents the old type of drover's breed known as the Smithfield because it was used to herd cattle and sheep in London's Smithfield meat market. It shows similarities with the working bearded collie of the Scottish Highlands and the French briard. Beneath a hirsute exterior the body is built for speed and endurance, which, added to the dog's innate keen intelligence, makes it valuable as a founding father in lurcher breeding.

Little serious attention was given to animal breeding (apart from horses) until the 1700s but then a number of country gentlemen became interested in livestock improvement, which included sporting dogs. Among them was Lord Orford, a keen zoologist who kept a private zoo on his Norfolk estate and enjoyed coursing above other sports. He aimed to bring scientific principles to the breeding of better greyhounds but was hampered by a lack of any contemporary knowledge of genetic inheritance, and so his 'science' was really a matter of picking out the best greyhounds and crossing them with a strange assortment of other breeds in order to improve their coursing ability – it would seem that greyhounds at that time had become too refined to be up to coursing a hare.

Evidently with the object of building a stronger skeletal structure he used a bulldog as a first cross and then put the best progeny back to an Italian greyhound to narrow the skull of the third generation. Another ingredient was the Norfolk lurcher, which was sensible, but, for some reason best known to himself, he also tried bloodhounds and had subsequent difficulty in breeding out this strain of strange beasts which hunted by scent, belling at the tops of their voices.

However, Lord Orford's endeavours must have met with some success because after his death in 1791 several of his greyhounds were bought by Colonel Thomas Thornton. These were taken to Yorkshire but, bred for the flatlands of Norfolk, they found the hills and dales of Northern England too difficult a terrain and were unable to twist and turn without suffering injury. Colonel Thornton crossed them with local rough haired greyhounds descended from now extinct wolfhounds, which although they were known as Yorkshire greyhounds were in fact, a type of lurcher, and kept the resultant strain until his death in 1823.

Organised coursing began in 1776 when the Swaffham Coursing Club was founded in Norfolk and this was followed sixty years later by the inauguration of the famous Waterloo Cup run at Sefton Altcar in Lancashire, but the National Coursing Club only came into being in 1858, when Rules were formulated which apply today. The Greyhound Stud Book was founded in 1882, listing the pedigrees of dogs and the names of their owners but the fashion for crossbreeding which had been so prevalent only a few years earlier suggests that some pedigrees may have been distinctly suspect; probably the greyhounds bred by Julyana Berners were of purer stock than those registered in the reign of Queen Victoria.

Lurchers continued to be bred and highly valued by their gypsy and poacher owners, who would be very surprised to find that what was considered by squires and their gamekeepers as a ragamuffin animal to be shot on sight, had now become a much sought-after dog which competes at coursing meetings and for prestigious prizes at shows organised in the grounds of stately homes. But in reality it is more surprising that it took so long for sportsmen to discover the worth of a good lurcher.

2 Lurcher Types Around the World

TYPES of dog resembling the English lurcher occur in many parts of the world and, since most of them breed true, they are of interest to those who hope to establish the lurcher as a breed in its own right rather than continue with the somewhat hit-and-miss crosses on which most breeders have to rely.

Kangaroo Dog

As its name implies, this is an Australian breed which was developed in the early 1800s to hunt kangaroos on outback properties. It has seldom been seen outside its native land, although the then Prince of Wales (later Edward VII) is known to have owned and exhibited one of these dogs in 1864.

Various breeds contributed to its development on the basis of the greyhound crossed with the old English staghounds and Irish wolfhounds and, presumably, any other available dogs. No doubt, ruthless culling dependant on an animal's efficiency as a hunter of kangaroos led to the production of a definite type conforming to a standard.

It is a muscular dog built on greyhound lines, with a long low-set tail. The average height is 71cm (28in); coat harsh and short; colour brindle, brindle and white, black and tan, black, tan and white.

Rampur Hound

This is an old established breed found in North West India, similar in appearance and size to the kangaroo dog but with a smooth, sleek coat. The most favoured colour is black but black-and-tan or blue-grey is permissible.

The Poligar hound found in the Madras area is similar to the Rampur hound, and is sometimes crossed with it.

Banjara Greyhound

These are smaller than Rampur hounds and come from Northern India. It may be considered as a typical lurcher type with a sort, rough coat. The average height is 69cm (27in); colour brindle, grey, sandy, or wheaten. It is not known in Britain but a few have been taken to the USA. Since the nomadic Banjara people are believed to be ancestors of European Romany families, it may be that these greyhounds contributed long ago to the early development of the lurcher.

Baganda Hunting Dog

Dogs of this breed are kept in packs by several Ugandan tribes and used for beating game out from scrub and elephant grass. The dogs are highly trained and run with a so-called 'king-dog' which wears a bell attached to its collar. They resemble a smaller version of the Indian Banjara greyhound, with an average height of 50cm (20in) and weighing 13.5kg (30–35lb). Colour yellowish tan or back and white. They are unknown outside East Africa.

South American Hunting Dogs

The primitive forest Indians of Brazil and northern Guyana keep domestic dogs of greyhound type, probably descendants of greyhounds imported by the Spanish conquistadors crossed with the wild Surinam dog (*Dusicyon thous*) which is common in many parts of tropical South America.

The dogs are highly prized for hunting, as objects for barter and, to some extent, as status symbols. These Indians are capable of considerable rapport with their animals and make very good dog trainers. Women of a tribe care for the dogs which are given every available comfort. The average height of a hunting dog is 58cm (23in); the coat is short and harsh; white with black markings. It has developed as a distinct breed but has not, as far as I know, ever been seen outside its native land.

American Coyote Hound

Game coursed in North America consists of cottontail rabbits and jack rabbits (both species of hare); the red fox and coyotes. Various pure and crossed breeds, including greyhounds, salukis and whippets, are used for all except the coyote, which, being a small wolf, is a fierce adversary and one which requires a fast powerful dog to kill it cleanly.

Since coyotes are a menace to farm stock they are hunted both for sport and for economic reasons, and this has led to the production of a distinct type of dog capable of coursing it over rough terrain for a distance of two miles or so. The majority of coyote hounds are bred from greyhounds crossed with deerhounds, Irish wolfhounds and borzois (known in the USA as Russian wolfhounds), and a programme of breeding 'back' and 'in and in' has resulted in the formation of a recognisable type which is well on the way to becoming a breed. This dog is between 71cm (28in) and 76cm (30in) in height; the coat is thick and wiry; colours vary from black to sandy.

3 Breeds that make Lurchers

A NUMBER of different pure breeds have been crossed to produce lurchers. As a rule the initial cross has been with a greyhound, although salukis have been used with some success; the objective being to create a fast sight hound which is more intelligent than an average member of the greyhound family. With this in mind, a greyhound/working collie bred lurcher is one of the best, which sometimes can be improved by the addition of a third, or even fourth breed provided that the greyhound image is not lost in the course of mongrelising succeeding generations of puppies: if cross-breeding is taken too far there is a risk of high 'wastage' in a litter in which some puppies revert to show undesirable characteristics inherited from a single ancestor. Equally, temperament can become a problem. A good looking lurcher which bites people or fights other dogs is worse than useless; yet, these traits are easily bred into a line from one ill-tempered parent or grandparent and so breeding lurchers should involve great care in the selection of individual dogs, not only for their appearance but also for their character.

Greyhounds

The modern greyhound is divided into three types: coursing, racing and show greyhounds. The first two are used for lurcher breeding but show greyhounds are now bred with an exaggerated bend of stifle and are both slower and more clumsy in the field than their counterparts.

A coursing greyhound is ideal as one parent of a lurcher and stud dogs are at a premium for this purpose. The choice of a racing greyhound needs more care. A big dog standing over a lot of ground looks impressive but it is well known in racing circles that a large, long greyhound is at a disadvantage against a shorter-coupled, smaller dog sprinting on a track with sharp bends although he (or she) may be faster on the straight. The same applies to such a dog tried for coursing: he tends to go too fast, over-running and possibly injuring himself while trying to turn at speed.

Salukis

These Arabian hounds trace back in virtually their present form to at least

5,000 BC and were used then, as now, for coursing either in a brace or working with a falcon. The particular quarry is gazelle which requires both speed and the ability to make fast turns. While people of the Moslem faith generally look upon dogs as unclean animals, the shieks who own salukis regard them as being in a class of their own with the same status as an Arab horse and a hunting falcon.

The coat is soft and silky, feathered on the ears, tail and legs. It is similar in size to a greyhound, varying from 51cm (20in) for a bitch to 71cm (28in) for a dog. Unlike a greyhound, it has drop ears.

It has been used with success as an alternative to a greyhound in breeding lurchers, but as a broad generalisation it may be said that salukis are inclined to be wilful and not to be trusted with sheep, and should be matched with a more tractable breed.

Slughis

This is a North African gazelle hound and closely related to salukis, but differs in having a short coat and a broader skull. It is used for hunting hare and fox as well as gazelle. While still uncommon in the West, there are now several kennels in Britain and North America and the breed may prove very useful as a lurcher cross.

Whippets

The origin of the whippet is a controversial subject. Certainly it was

Minnie. A small smooth lurcher of whippet size. Her breeding is unknown but her appearance and height suggests that there were whippets in her ancestry. This type is popular in the USA for coursing cotton-tail and jack rabbits, and is often described as a 'cold-blood' to differentiate between it and a pedigree greyhound or whippet. In particular the hind-quarters of this bitch illustrate a good bend of stifle and low-set hocks which are desirable features in a fast lurcher.

developed in Yorkshire by miners who used these dogs for rabbit coursing and for racing, and it seems likely that it is descended from initial crosses between small greyhounds, the old English white terrier (now extinct) and the Manchester terrier, but, whatever its forebears may have been, the modern whippet has the graceful outline of a greyhound and is astonishingly fast over a distance of two hundred and fifty metres, and has the added advantage of a much more placid temperament than its larger counterpart which is liable to fight when excited. It is excellent for rabbiting and will course and catch hares with ease, but in the latter case, because of its comparatively small size, has difficulty in making a clean kill – anyone who has heard a hare crying *in extremis* will be deterred from hunting hares for the pot with a whippet.

As a cross for breeding smaller lurchers the whippet has everything to recommend it. Suitable crosses include Welsh sheepdog, small greyhound and Bedlington terrier.

Italian Greyhounds

These are true miniature greyhounds and of ancient lineage: they were known to the kings of Egypt and widely kept by the Romans who probably brought them to Gaul and Britain. From the Renaissance until the eighteenth century the Italian was built on the lines of a whippet, but in Victorian times fanciers began to select only the smallest, most 'elegant' specimens with the result that the breed deteriorated to become a ladies' lapdog. Unfortunately, the trend persists today but size varies, even within a litter, and it is possible to find dogs weighing 5.5kg (12lb) or more which are keen and efficient rabbiters. Since they possess greyhound temperament as well as speed, a cross with a whippet will create a more mellow character, which can be further improved by tripartite breeding with a small collie to make a good small lurcher.

Ibizan Hound

Although little known in Britain before the 1960s Ibizan hounds are becoming increasingly popular as show and sporting dogs. Like other members of the greyhound family, it is an old breed dating from the Ancient Egyptians who depicted it in *bas relief* and in statuettes to represent the dog god Anubis. It is thought to have been brought to its native Balearic Islands by the Phoenicians, and it is still used there for rabbit and hare coursing.

It is generally red or yellow and white in colour; the coat may be smooth or rough; the average height around 64cm (25in). These dogs are very fast and active – one I owned jumped a fence 3 metres high from what the Irish call 'a standing lep'. The Ibizan appears to offer good prospects for lurcher breeders: it is a keen worker and has a kind temperament.

Afghan Hound

The modern show-bred Afghan is a galumphing fool quite useless as a progenitor of lurchers. This is a sad state of affairs for a hunting breed which existed in Afghanistan more than 2,000 years BC, but nowadays it is intractable and more disposed to hunt sheep than course legitimate quarry.

Borzois

While the borzoi, known as the Russian wolfhound in the USA, is perhaps the most spectacular greyhound breed, it is not suited to the work of an English lurcher, although it has been used in the development of the American coyote hound. Its minimum height is 74cm (29in) but many are bigger than this.

This completes the list of true greyhounds, some more suitable than others as ingredients in the making of lurchers. The next consideration is suitable crosses and pre-eminent among these are Scottish deerhounds and working collies.

Deerhounds

This charming hound has everything to recommend it as a lurcher parent: highly intelligent, fast and silent in its work; yet docile and showing great devotion at home. The breed has natural dignity and those who know it recognise the faraway, wistful look which is inherited by its lurcher progeny.

A deerhound bitch is best mated to a greyhound, rather than the other way round when the puppies might prove rather large at birth. Other successful crosses include greyhound/collie lurchers, but, whatever the cross, the resultant puppies are likely to be large lurchers measuring between 71cm (28in) and 76cm (30in), with the rough coat and grey, wheaten or brindle colour of the deerhound.

Border Collies

Although sheepdogs of various breeds and types date from time immemorial, the trial-bred collie is a comparatively new breed renowned for its intelligence and obedience to instructions. Its characteristics are speed, stamina over rough terrain, and the instinctive 'clapping' and 'eyeing' behaviour seen when it is working sheep: the dog 'claps' (lies down and inches forward), using stealth to move the sheep, while it 'eyes' them with the fixed stare of the predator. This behaviour is not seen in other collie breeds and it is thought that some pointer or setter blood was introduced during the nineteenth century to trigger this action.

Floss. The author's trial-bred sheepdog is an example of the best type of collie used for crossing with greyhounds or whippets to produce mainly smooth puppies (although a few with wiry hair occur in such litters). These crosses have the advantage of stamina, intelligence and an inbred response to careful training.

It is not a big dog, usually about 51cm (20in) in height; the coat is dense and weatherproof, shorter on the face and legs and thickest on the long, low-set tail. The usual colour is black and white, but some are more white than black and others may be black and tan, tricolour or blue merle.

When crossed with a greyhound the majority of collie bitches produce either smooth or wiry coated puppies. They make very good mothers.

I have emphasised the use of trial-bred *sheep* dogs to underline the importance of not trying to breed lurchers from the rowdy, noisy type of cattle dog commonly found on farms, which are all very well for driving a mob of bullocks, biting and barking as they go, but they have no place in the parentage of sensible, silent lurchers.

German Shepherd Dogs (Alsatians)

These intelligent shepherd dogs have proved themselves in many kinds of work but until recent times have seldom been used in lurcher breeding. Nowadays the major drawback to the alsatian is that it has been bred for the show-ring with an exaggerated bend of stifle which, in part at least, has led to a high incidence of hip-displasia – an inherited deformity. However, the types used by the police and military have proved successful when bred with a greyhound, particularly those bred back to a greyhound in the second generation.

Great Dane

I have known only one greyhound/great Dane lurcher, a very handsome 'tiger-striped' brindle measuring about 74cm (29in), and according to her owner fast and keen, killing both foxes and hares.

Bedlington terrier

This breed originated with gypsies and was a type of lurcher used for rabbiting and also for fighting. It is thought to have been developed from crosses including whippets, Dandie Dinmonts and otter hounds, but this must be largely conjecture since it has been in existence for at least two centuries. The modern dog measures about 40cm (16in) and is found in several colours – blue being the most popular. It matches well with a whippet, which is probably the best cross as this tends to quench an otherwise somewhat fiery temperament inherited from its fighting ancestors. Unlike most terriers, it is silent as befits a one-time lurcher.

A number of other breeds have been crossed with greyhounds to make so-called lurchers. Among these are retrievers and foxhounds, but few purists would accept these as lurchers and, furthermore, the progeny of such crosses are likely to be too slow for coursing (using scent rather than sight) and liable to give tongue in pursuit of a quarry – a cardinal sin where a lurcher is concerned.

Smithfield dogs

It is generally agreed that a shaggy type of drovers' dog is part ancestor to many so-called Norfolk lurchers. This 'Smithfield' dog both herded cattle and sheep from the eastern counties of England to London and worked in

Whisky. This well-known dog is of Smithfield descent and much sought after as a sire. There is some argument for and against white colouration in lurchers: there is a faction who believe them to be too visible at night but, in fact, a pied dog is better camouflaged than a black one in all but total darkness.

Emma. This young daughter of Whisky is white with blue markings probably inherited from deerhound blood on her dam's side. The width of brisket and depth of chest prove her staying power, while the vertical line from the pinbones of the pelvis to the toes of the hind feet show that she is fast.

the meat market there, hence the name Smithfield. Although many people assume that it is now extinct, mongrel dogs of the same type frequently occur and, sadly, many of them end up in dogs homes, unwanted because of their size and tangly coats. The originals probably stemmed from the same root stock as the Old English bobtail and the bearded collie – the latter is very similar to a Smithfield in build but rather smaller, lurchers of known Smithfield descent are still highly valued as among the most intelligent workers and dogs of considerable stature.

4 Choosing a Puppy

THE growing popularity of the lurcher has meant that any number of long-legged mongrel puppies are advertised as lurchers, deceiving novice buyers who are sadly disillusioned when an animal grows up to resemble a pi-dog of the sort found scrounging garbage from Cairo to Singapore. Such puppies are given spurious parentage to snare the unwary and so it is important not to buy unless, at least, the dam is available for inspection and, better still, both parents can be seen; and if suspicion remains, check by her behaviour and signs of recent lactation that the bitch really is the mother of a particular litter. Of course, when a source is obviously respectable and the vendor is an established breeder these precautions are unnecessary, but many handsome true lurchers may be found in rough and ready surroundings, such as caravan sites and scrap yards, and so can

Molly. A yearling deerhound/greyhound cross. This nice bitch is primarily a family pet but enjoys opportunities to course rabbits in fields around her country home. Her life style offers an example of the adaptability of lurchers, as she spends part of her time in a London flat with her owners, taking exercise in public parks. One problem which can beset lurcher owners walking their dogs in city parks is that bye-laws may prohibit greyhound-types from running free without a muzzle; this is because on a few sad occasions toy dogs, such as pomeranians, have been coursed and killed by unruly greyhounds.

rogues intent on hoodwinking a naïve buyer into taking home a 'bargain'.

The next consideration is temperament: the parents of a litter and any other adult dogs present should behave with detached politeness to a stranger, showing neither aggressive nor idiotically effusive behaviour; while the puppies should respond to an offered hand by wagging and coming to have a sniff. My own experience has shown that puppies which scrabble at the sides of their pen, yipping and squealing when a stranger appears are likely to grow up to become stupid adult dogs that prove difficult to train. A sensible puppy shows some reserve until it is reassured and justified in wagging and wriggling with pleasure at being petted, but at this stage, again think twice about the puppy which proceeds to bite hard and tear at clothing instead of licking a stroking hand. Lastly, and it hardly needs mentioning, avoid a puppy which lurks in the background, clearly nervous and unwilling to come forward.

The litter as whole should be reasonably level in size and conformation, bearing in mind that cross- and tripartite breeding will result in some differences in size, as for example in the case of puppies which have greyhound, whippet and Bedlington forebears. Inspect the pen in which the puppies are kept: it should be clean and show no signs of diarrhoea – if it does, go home. One is often attracted to a particular puppy and, all else being equal, the choice is settled there and then, but sometimes two or three may appeal and the litter needs weeding out to find the one and only.

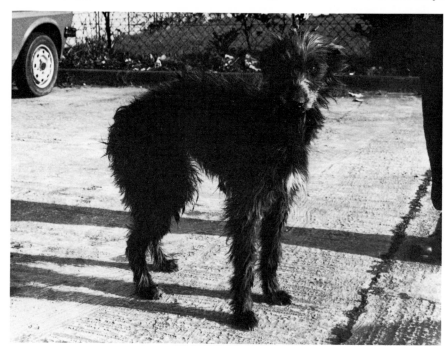

Jessie. This bitch shows a reversion to the hairiness of one Smithfield grandparent and is not in herself very attractive, but she has potential for breeding good lurchers when matched with a greyhound or deerhound cross.

Assuming that the buyer has a preconceived notion about which sex is required, either all the bitches or all the dog puppies should be removed to allow a better view of the remainder, and these should be followed by other discards until the choice is reduced to, say, two.

A lurcher puppy at the age of eight to ten weeks should be forward in growth, with good bone and substance – often the joints of a well-boned puppy may seem *slightly* disproportionately large but these will fine down to give a big adult animal. Since a baby lurcher is, or should be, a pudgy little creature, its outline is not readily seen, but if a hand is placed under its belly and gently pressed upwards the depth of chest will be more apparent, and also show the stance of the hind legs: future speed can be recognised when the toes of the hind feet are in line with the pin-bones on the croup above the root of the tail. It may be difficult to gauge the length of neck, but it is easier to see good sloping shoulders and straight front legs.

A physical check-up is the next stage for a chosen puppy, working from nose to tail. The teeth should be white and level, the gums a healthy pink and the breath sweet, the eyes clean and sparkling; there should be plenty of flesh along the spine (a thin spine and a pot-belly indicate an infestation of roundworms). Part the coat to look for spots of blotches on the skin resulting from flea or louse bites; then look at the navel for umbilical hernia (a small lump is harmless but one the size of a hazel nut or larger may cause problems), and check the scrotum of a dog puppy to insure that both testes have descended – a retained testicle can be the source of a cancerous growth in later life. Rickets is seldom found nowadays but if a puppy's birthplace and early care leaves something to be desired, it is worth feeling the ribs for tell-tale nodules on the bones and, of course, for the least sign of bandiness in the legs. A friendly puppy which passes these tests has every prospect of making a good lurcher.

I have not mentioned coat texture because this varies according to a puppy's breeding. My own preference is for the short wiry coat of the classic lurcher, with slightly longer hair on the jaws to give a suggestion of moustache and beard: this type of coat is more weather-proof and protects the skin from superficial damage from thorns and such. A drawback to Bedlington blood is that this can produce a linty coat, soft to the touch and easily soaked in wet weather. Smooth-haired lurchers of sheepdog descent inherit a thicker coat than their greyhound 'other halves' and this gives them better protection from the weather.

As to the sex to choose, there is a general concensus of opinion that among the greyhound family the female is deadlier than the male, and certainly this seems to be true for bitch whippets which are usually keener on coursing than dogs. The disadvantage to a bitch is that she is out of action for three weeks every six months or so when she is in season, but the advantage to set against this is her ability to found a dynasty for an owner interested in breeding his or her own line of lurchers.

Amber. A gypsy-bred whippet/terrier bitch. After stealing an unsuitable mating and producing a litter of mongrels with some difficulty, she was spayed and now shows the almost inevitable fattening effect of this operation in spite of a strict diet and plenty of exercise.

Buying an adult lurcher

It is easy to be tempted by an advertisement offering a fully-trained lurcher but very few genuine dogs come onto the market and so it is vital to check the reason for sale. Acceptable reasons include bereavement or an owner who really is going abroad or moving to a city apartment, or even one that has gone bankrupt or to jail. Nobody else is likely to sell a 'ready-made' lurcher unless it has one or more bad habits, such as sheep worrying, eating the quarry it kills, or going off on lone hunting expeditions; not to mention biting children and fighting other dogs. Furthermore, a lurcher is usually a one-man dog and there may be great difficulty in persuading it to transfer its allegiance to a new owner. All things considered, therefore, my advice is to think twice and yet again before buying a full-grown lurcher.

5 Foods and Feeding

A NOURISHING and appetising diet is all important in rearing and maintaining a lurcher in good condition. Food consists of protein, carbohydrates and fat, plus necessary vitamins and minerals, and an owner needs to understand the functions of these nutrients in order to provide a dog with a diet suited to its stages of growth as a puppy and then to its energy requirements as an adult. Energy in this context means not only running but also the replacement of tissue and worn spare parts.

Contrary to a common belief, the dog is not a strict carnivore by nature but (like humans) an omnivore with a partiality for meat. I have kept two kinds of wild dog, a dingo and a small Asian species, and found that while both were incapable of digesting cereals and cooked meats intended for domestic dogs, they relished green and root vegetables and fruit fed raw. A ration consisting of twenty-five per cent vegetables and fruit and seventy-five per cent meat protein including eggs maintained them in excellent condition. A domestic dog, on the other hand, has thousands of years of association with man behind it and thrives on a reverse ratio – that is, twenty-five per cent meat. As an example, at one time I knew a pair of German shepherd dogs (Alsatians) which were kept as guards in a knacker's yard, helping themselves to meat at will but not otherwise fed, and both were obviously unfit with staring coats and poor physique due to this unbalanced diet.

Proteins

The dog is geared to animal protein and gains little if any benefit from vegetable protein, such as soya. Suitable animal products are muscle meat, offal, fish, eggs, milk and hard cheese. Nutrients of this kind are used for growth, to build up muscle and renew wear and tear. A dog which receives too little protein will draw on reserves within its body and fail to thrive, while conversely, too much protein puts a strain on the kidneys and in excess can cause toxic substances to be absorbed into the blood stream if it is given in the form of meat alone – as in the case of the knacker's alsatians.

Carbohydrates

These may be considered as fuel, producing energy and heat. Some is laid down as a reserve of fat in the body: a resource used during times of high activity and in cold weather, and by a bitch suckling puppies. Carbohydrates are mainly supplied by wholemeal biscuits or brown bread, or in hunt kennels in the form of a pudding made from cooked oatmeal or flaked maize.

Fats

Milk is a prime source of fat, which is also found as fat attached to muscle meat, as suet and in cod-liver oil. It functions as a source of concentrated energy, and is useful in building up the type of greyhound lurcher which has a tendency to look like a toast-rack, and also for dogs working in cold, wet weather. In winter my own working dogs were each given a walnut-sized piece of suet (obtained from the fat surrounding a sheep's kidney) which was crumbled and sprinkled on their food.

Vitamins

While vitamins are divided and sub-divided on an alphabetical system only four need concern the dog owner and these are, *vitamin A* which promotes growth in a young dog and renewal in an adult; it is found in egg yolk, milk, cod-liver oil and liver. A deficiency stunts growth and reduces a dog's natural resistance to disease. *Vitamin B* again affects growth in the young, and also the nervous system and heart, and is important in the conversion of carbohydrates. It is present in red meat, liver, eggs and yeast. Deficiency stunts growth and can lead to nervous disorders and eczema. *Vitamin D* is valuable as a catalyst, acting to aid the absorption of the minerals calcium and phosphate. The main sources are eggs, meat juices, milk, cod-liver oil and sunshine. A deficiency will reduce the strength of a dog's bone structure and, in severe cases, can cause rickets. *Vitamin E* was, until recent years, considered only as a means of increasing fertility but it is now recognised as necessary for growth and maintenance of the skeleton and muscles. It is found in several foods including wheatmeal biscuits and liver; dark-fleshed fish such as herrings tend to suppress vitamin E. A deficiency can cause sterility in both dogs and bitches.

Minerals

The two important dietry minerals are calcium and phosphorus: both are essential for building bones and teeth and are involved in the action of muscles and the clotting of blood. They are found in milk and eggs or may be given in the form of a mineral supplement such as Stress or Vetzyme yeast tablets, which also contain the essential vitamin D that allows the

Variation within a litter
is clearly illustrated by
these sisters, the result of
a cross between a
deerhound/greyhound
sire and a greyhound/
sheepdog dam.

mineral to be absorbed. The addition of milk and eggs to the diet will not overload the system with minerals but a too heavy handed use of supplements can result in the formation of bladder stones, so the recommended dosage should be followed exactly according to the size and weight of a puppy or dog.

Dog foods

The basic diet of most dogs is biscuit meal and this should be selected with care. Meal produced by reputable manufacturers is likely to be a good nourishing food but I view with some distrust bulk meals sold as 'hound meal' or 'terrier meal' without a brand name – they may be cheaper but the feeding value is questionable in many instances.

The local knacker who slaughters old, injured or sick farm animals and horses, provides a cheap source of meat but there are drawbacks: the law insists that such meat is subjected to steam cooking at a high temperature to kill possible germs and this incidentally removes a considerable amount of nutrients. Furthermore, a diseased animal may have been dosed with drugs before death. This leads me to suggest that the use of knacker's meat is a false economy.

However, there are valuable cheap foods available and one of the best is sheeps' paunches, which can be obtained by arrangement with an abbatoir. A raw paunch is a fairly revolting object, resembling a dirty sodden bath towel with its own distinctive stench which increases during cooking, and this may deter more sensitive people. But it is a gourmet dish for a dog and who are we to be disgusted when we enjoy Camembert cheese and hung game. Paunches should be rinsed under cold running water and then boiled until soft, when it can be cut into small pieces and mixed with meal. The very smelly 'soup' should be thrown out and the meal moistened with milk or gravy instead. This food is suitable only for adult dogs and may be given, say, four times a week, allowing more varied meals on the remaining three days.

Other by-products of the butchery trade which, when cooked, make nourishing meals include:

COW UDDER: Like paunches, udders are not available at butchers' shops but can be obtained by arrangement with an abbatoir. It is cellular material, the meat whitish in colour, and it usually contains some residue of milk. Udder should be boiled until soft and then either cut in pieces or minced; the milky soup is valuable and can be used to moisten the food. It should be considered as an occasional treat.

OX CHEEK: Cattle are equipped with powerful facial muscles to enable them to chew the cud, and this type of beef makes an excellent and comparatively cheap form of red meat for dogs; it can be fed raw or cooked with its own juices and is suitable for dogs of all ages including weaned puppies – it is too sinewy for very young puppies. Since this is clean meat it can be sold in a butcher's shop.

All the following are also obtainable from a butcher:

MELT: This is a trade term for the spleen of cattle and sheep. Since it is connected with the blood supply, it makes a rich dark soup when boiled and this is enjoyed by all dogs, but few will eat it raw and most will vomit if they do.

SHEEP'S HEAD: A head should be sawn, not chopped, in half lengthways (chopping can leave dangerous slivers of bone hidden in the flesh), and complete with brain and tongue. It should be boiled until the meat falls off the bone; the rather insipid soup can be improved by the addition of a stock cube, such as Oxo or Bovril, or some root vegetables – carrots or turnips – to give a better flavour.

HEART: Sheep and ox hearts, boiled and fed with the soup, are very appetising for adult dogs, but prove indigestible to puppies and elderly lurchers.

OX LIVER: Liver from cattle is cheaper than other forms and the less saleable parts containing 'tubes' are suitable for dogs. It is a valuable source of vitamins but the problem is that much of the vitamin content is destroyed by cooking, yet when fed raw in more than small amounts almost always induces vomiting. The answer is to use a little raw liver, cut small, mixed with other food, and to cook the remainder for only a short time. It sometimes happens that a young lurcher (a sapling in greyhound parlance) can become a faddy feeder while it is cutting its adult teeth or shortly afterwards, and if this is not due to illness, cooked liver will often trigger a renewed appetite – the average dog of any breed would sell its soul for fried liver.

GIBLETS: Butchers and poulterers sometimes offer the offal from chickens, ducks, turkeys and geese under this collective term which describes liver, heart, gizzard and neck. Gizzards should be cut open and cleared of their content of fibre and grit, and the whole lot can then be boiled and fed with the delicious stock.

RABBIT: The owner of a lurcher is likely to be well supplied with rabbits and these make an excellent cheap food if cooked until the bones can be easily extracted from the flesh. It is vital to remove every last bone as these can be lethal if swallowed.

Neither rabbit nor sheep meat of any kind should be fed raw because the smell will encourage a dog to eat rather than retrieve a killed rabbit, and, worse, a taste for raw mutton may lead to sheep worrying.

EGGS: As I have made clear earlier, eggs form an important part of a dog's diet, but for anyone who does not keep fowls at home this can prove an expensive item. However, it is usually possible to obtain cracked eggs from a poultry farm at a cheap rate on the basis of a standing order. Large lurchers will benefit from up to a dozen raw eggs over a period of a week; smaller types about six.

MILK: This is equally valuable and, given a choice, goat's milk is the best as it is higher in protein, carbohydrate and fat content, and the smaller fat globules tend to remain suspended rather than rising to form cream at the top. If facilities are available it is well worth keeping a goat, particularly for anyone intending to breed lurchers: a pedigree dairy goat is likely to go on lactating for two years after one kidding, and any billy kids she may produce can be slaughtered to make useful meat for the dogs.

CHEESE: This is a substance enjoyed by man, beast, bird and even some fish, and is a useful additive to a dog's diet, not only providing a pleasant taste but also valuable protein. Hard, Cheddar type, cheese can often be wheedled from a friendly grocer who has pieces of rind and crumbled bits to spare, which can be chopped or grated over prepared food.

HONEY: Honey is seldom given to dogs, if only because of its high price, but a spoonful dissolved in warm milk is good for lactating bitches, for any dog recovering from illness and for lurchers using a lot of energy.

As a collector of old dog books I am especially fond of one author, Colonel G.H.Badcock, who wrote and broadcast in the early 1930s on the subject of dogs in general and dog training in particular. His kennel of gundogs were fed an exclusive diet of whole boiled herrings and brown bread, which says much for the stamina of retrievers and spaniels of that era. Research has shown that while herrings and the like have a high protein and oil content, as a food these fish have the effect of inhibiting the absorption of essential vitamins which makes them most unsuitable for dog feeding — quite apart from the presence of innumerable potentially choking bones. However, various kinds of white fish can be fed to dogs to provide variety in the diet, or in hot, humid conditions when a dog may lack appetite for meat but appreciate cold boiled fish. Boiled or steamed fish is also good for building up a bitch which has recently weaned a litter, and for convalescents.

FISH: Since even coley, once considered only as a suitable dinner for a cat, is now expensive the alternative is dog fish, species of small shark which are sometimes given the unlikely title of 'rock salmon'. This is a good dog food and has the added advantage of being virtually boneless. On the subject of bones, the flesh of any other sort of fish must be searched to remove every last bone because one can pierce the intestine and result in the death of a dog.

Animal bones and those from poultry can be equally lethal. This may seem nonsensical when wild carnivores eat their prey bones and all, but those bones are raw and spiky kinds are left for the attention of crows or vultures. Cooking alters the structure of bones and this makes them liable to crack into sharp splinters when gnawed; which leaves a dog owner with only one safe but valuable bone and that is beef shin.

BEEF SHIN BONES: Gnawing a tough, marrow-filled bone not only provides a satisfying occupation for a dog, particularly if it has to be left

Penny. A greyhound X whippet/sheepdog, she is her master's sole companion: ready to catch his supper or follow at his heels to market or the local pub or stretch out on the hearth rug. Her value to him is beyond price.

alone in its owner's absence, but also serves to keep the teeth clean and to aid digestion. The bone should be sawn, not chopped, to give a straight length of about 15cm (6in) so that marrow is available at either end. It will remain as a possession valued by a dog for some time but is best replaced every week or so.

VEGETABLES: Either cooked or raw, these are enjoyed by most dogs and represent an important part of the diet. In fact, a dog likes the equivalent of the human 'meat and two veg' course, replacing potatoes with biscuit meal but not forgetting the gravy; or in summer cold meat and salad. Although some dogs, including my own, will chew up raw cabbage, lettuce and carrots fed separately, besides appreciating vegetables cooked as part of a stew, in most cases raw vegetables are best given chopped and mixed with the meat and biscuit feed.

FRUIT: This must be considered as a titbit: too much can have an aperient effect. Dogs vary in their liking for fruit but a number enjoy sweet apple, pear and berries such as strawberries and raspberries, and some have a passion for banana. A whippet/sheepdog lurcher of mine learned to pick hedgerow blackberries for herself and, unfortunately, advanced from there to take soft fruit from bushes and the strawberry bed in the garden.

Using a deep freezer

Until the advent of the home freezer cooking for dogs was a considerable chore, but now it is possible to freeze bags of ready-cooked food in quantities to make enough for one or two meals for a single dog or for several. Cooked food can be plain meat in its gravy or a stew of meat and vegetables, either of which can be boiled up from the frozen state and then allowed to cool to an edible temperature. Frozen meat such as ox cheek should be thawed over-night, before feeding raw or cooked. Offal has a short freezer life and ought not to be kept more than a month or so. I would hesitate to include paunches in the household freezer but if the number of dogs warrants a kennel freezer then raw paunches will keep satisfactorily for several months.

Convenience foods

Most of us rely on convenience foods to some extent because they are convenient. Those sold under well known brand names are palatable and reasonably nutritious but, in my opinion, do not compare with fresh foods prepared at home and, furthermore, they are expensive. These ready-made feeds fall into three main categories: canned meat, semi-moist packaged meat and dry 'complete diets'.

CANNED MEAT: The contents of cans depend on price: cheaper products contain a percentage of cereal and texturised vegetable matter, while others which appear meaty largely consist of jelly — which can be discovered by heating an opened can. Reputable firms which employ a staff of veterinary scientists and have established their own kennels for research, offer reliable foods at a cost.

SEMI-MOIST MEAT: This varies in content but is likely to contain a proportion of vegetable protein. The product is kept moist in a package by the addition of a chemical known as a humectant.

COMPLETE DRY DIETS After being on the market for some twenty years, manufacturers have devised several complete diets in pellet and flake form which are widely used by pet owners, commercial kennels, greyhound trainers, and for police and army dogs. The type intended for greyhounds should prove suitable for a working lurcher. I believe that dogs thrive on this diet but my reservations are based on two points: first, fresh meat in its own juices must be better, and, second, mealtime is the highlight of a dog's day and it is a drab prospect if the same dinner turns up week in week out, the taste predictable every time.

Feeding a weaned puppy

A lurcher puppy will usually arrive in its new home at the age of about nine weeks, by which time it should have been completely weaned for more than a fortnight and accustomed to a mixed diet of meat, cereals and milk. Since lurchers vary so much in size it is impossible to generalise about the amount of food it will require (as one could with a pure bred puppy such as a Bedlington): each feed should be enough to satisfy without bloating it, and from eight to twelve weeks old the puppy needs five feeds a day which can be conveniently spaced as breakfast, lunch, tea, supper and a final meal last thing at night. These should consist of three solid and two liquid feeds and are best given as:

> Breakfast – warm milk with beaten-up raw egg.
> Lunch (midday) – meat and puppy grade biscuit meal moistened with stock or milk.
> Tea – warm milk.
> Supper – the same as lunch.
> Late snack – a small ration of raw meat.

The reason for giving raw meat late at night is to keep the puppy content over a comparatively long time and avoid loading its bladder with liquid – although it must be given access to fresh drinking water at all times.

As a puppy grows the number of feeds should be reduced while the quantity is increased until at six months old it is getting two main meals a day. It will benefit from between one teaspoonful to one dessert spoonful of cod-liver oil, Vetzyme yeast tablets and a potentially big dog may need extra calcium in the form of calcium and vitamin D tablets. Milk and eggs remain important ingredients in the diet. It sometimes happens that a puppy proved not to be suffering from worms, will take to eating earth and filth at about the time it is cutting its adult teeth, and this can be a symptom of vitamin/mineral deficiency or the result of a too refined diet which may not give a dog's powerful 'gastric juices' enough to work on. It takes judgement to supply a nourishing diet which will promote growth and yet discourage dirty eating habits; a satisfactory answer is to include a proportion of offal and paunch to give variety, not forgetting beef shin marrow bones.

Those who prefer to feed canned meat to puppies will find that many reliable manufacturers produce special puppy food. Best quality canned meats intended for cats are an alternative – these are of higher animal protein content than standard dog foods.

Feeding a newly-arrived puppy is straightforward if it has been reared at home by the breeder, who will provide a diet sheet showing the system of feeding to which it is accustomed. But its initial care is more complicated if it has been bred and reared in a haphazard fashion by gypsies or other travelling people: in this case a carefully balanced diet at first may result in gastric upsets and such a puppy needs to be acclimatised to a proper diet (and, obviously should be treated against roundworms as a matter of course).

Feeding an adult dog

Larger types of lurcher are not adult until they are eighteen months old, and part-bred deerhounds may not be fully mature before they are two years old. Good body-building foods are all important for them in order to encourage a sturdy skeleton and muscular development. Part-whippet lurchers mature faster but still need a high quality diet for more than a year to produce the stamina required of a working dog.

There are two schools of thought relating to how often a dog should be fed: some people insist that two feeds a day are essential, but for many years now I have fed my dogs only once a day in the early evening. This settles them down to rest and sleep through the night after an appetising meal which is provided at five pm almost without fail (allowing for an occasional unavoidable delay). I am convinced of the value of punctual mealtimes: dogs are well aware of time and as the dinner hour approaches their bodies are geared to eat and digest with the aid of increased salivation. On the other hand, a dog that literally doesn't know where its next meal is coming from, will be anxious as its hunger grows and is liable to take to begging and thieving.

A companion lurcher given normal exercise, including the chance to hunt a few rabbits whenever possible, will thrive on a meat and biscuit diet, with added milk and eggs; but feeding the evening before a day's coursing should be different, giving the dog easily digested food which will be eliminated in the morning. Chopped raw meat is best, with some

A minor drawback to black lurchers is that the face is inclined to become grizzled white in early middle age, making a dog look older than its years.

milk and raw egg. Early on the day a raw egg may be given to satisfy an appetite which will be 'sharp set' after the night before's reduced feed of meat without biscuits.

The life span of a healthy member of the greyhound family is longer than many other breeds, often reaching the age of sixteen or more years, and with the onset of old age it is sensible to revise the diet, reverting to two feeds a day so as not to overload the digestive system.

WATER: A supply of fresh clean water is essential for a dog. Thirsty animals are unable to digest their food properly, and this can cause gastric and kidney complaints. Moreover, a dog which is suffering from thirst may drink polluted water and poison itself.

6 General Management

IT is an odd facet of human nature that so many owners of sporting dogs appear to take pride in their animal's ability to withstand neglect; yet no-one in his right mind would stable a tired, wet hunter without grooming it and providing a rug and a warming feed. The fact is that a well-kept dog is likely to have a longer useful life as a working companion than its neglected counterpart, which is almost certain to degenerate in middle age because of rheumatism and general wear and tear. My own dogs are given that little bit of extra care and, barring accidents, have a life expectancy of fourteen or more active years – at the moment I have a seventeen year-old terrier which is as lively as a cricket apart from a fluctuating amount of deafness, dependent, as it is in elderly humans, on her wish to hear. General management, then, covers the care of a dog from puppyhood to old age.

Blue. While this eight-month old puppy is mainly descended from greyhound/deerhound crosses, a Bedlington terrier grandparent has bequeathed a rather soft coat and woolly topknot on the head. The use of Bedlingtons in lurcher breeding is controversial: these dogs were developed by gypsies in the north of England both for hunting for the pot and for pit fighting, and although the appearance of a modern pedigree Bedlington has changed beyond all recognition, it still retains a strong hunting instinct and, unfortunately, a tendency to fight, which is a most undesirable trait in a lurcher.

The puppy

Plans should be made in advance before a puppy arrives in its new home, deciding where it is to sleep and where it is to spend its days, particularly at times when it has to be left unsupervised. The owner must remember that its first few days (and nights) are going to be bewildering for a puppy bereft of its mother and litter mates and the familiar sights, smells and sounds of its birthplace, and it needs kindness and understanding in order to settle happily with strangers.

Since a young puppy sleeps for a total of about eighteen out of each twenty-four hours, its bed is important: a basket is useless as this will be quickly demolished, and I prefer a hard plastic bed with a piece of old carpet cut to fit the base and covered with a blanket. Grey army blankets, obtainable from surplus stores, can be cut in half or quarters depending on size. The bed should be in a warm but not stuffy place where the puppy can rest comfortably and do the minimum amount of damage when it is active, and this suggests that a kitchen is the best site if it has a tiled or lino floor impervious to the inevitable pool. It is courting disaster to leave a puppy alone with upholstered chairs, cushions, books and anything else which is tearable, and while it is in its instinctively destructive stage the animal is not to blame if it wreaks havoc – this stage is an inheritance from

Even if a puppy such as this is well up to size it should not be allowed to take more than an easy rabbit now and again until it is over a year old. Exhausting exercise can spoil a young dog.

prehistoric wild dogs whose pups were given whole prey to dismember as part of their education as hunters.

Later, when destructive tendencies have ceased and the dog is outgrowing its puppy bed, a large bean-bag bed is ideal for a lurcher which likes to vary its sleeping attitude between curling up and lying full-length. These beds, packed with plastic 'beans', are warm and comfortable, and light to transport; there are several makes on the market with little to choose between them, provided that the chosen one has an easily removable cover which can be washed – most firms supply an extra cover to allow for this. Some dogs, confronted with a bean-bag for the first time, are hesitant about using this type of bed but will soon accept it if a familiar blanket is laid on top.

The provision of toys is perhaps a twee way of putting it but by this I mean giving the puppy objects to both occupy it and help its teeth. Cardboard cartons are good as things to be torn up with satisfying rending sounds and a beef shin bone, complete with marrow, is appetising and excellent for teething, and occupies a puppy when it is put to bed at night: contentedly chewing until it is overtaken by sleep instead of whimpering and keeping the whole family awake. The larger types of hide chews, sold by pet stores, can be used as well as real bones but should not entirely replace them as the veterinary profession believe that in some circumstances constantly chewing rawhide can lead to bladder stones. Do not give a lurcher puppy a rubber ball or ring to play with because this may encourage a hard mouth when it is an adult and required to retrieve game.

Play and sleep are equally important: playing develops muscles and a puppy's agility as it lollops about, tears up cardboard or busies itself with a bone, but the best playmate is another puppy or dog of a similar stature prepared to indulge in mock battles and chases round the garden. Dogs playing together should have their collars removed because it has been known for one to strangle accidentally the other by gripping and twisting its collar; in fact, I am against puppies wearing collars at home except for periods each day to accustom them to the feel of a leather band round the neck, but otherwise a collar may be a hazard and its constant wear can damage the hair follicles to leave a rough line on the throat. It must be born in mind throughout a lurcher's life that its greyhound neck is vulnerable to injury: a young puppy should start with a soft ordinary dog collar and transfer to a wide one as soon as its old enough.

A puppy tired by playing must be able to toddle off to its bed and sleep undisturbed by other animals or children. Rest allows the digestive processes to provide the nutrients needed for its growth – the best way to make a weedy dog is to deprive it of sleep when it is a puppy. While a bone is occupational therapy for a puppy at night, it may still voice its loneliness in an otherwise silent house and in this case is often soothed by the loud ticking of an old-fashioned alarm clock or a radio tuned low to an all-night

Tip. The author's whippet X Welsh sheepdog at the age of four months. This proved an excellent cross: she was fast and highly intelligent, and yet obedient by nature.

music programme: either blots out the worrying silence which suggests that it has been abandoned. If crying persists the puppy may be cold, which can be checked by feeling whether or not its ears and lower legs are warm, or hungry for rather more meat than it was given for its final meal of the day. Patience, even if it is hard come by late at night, is essential: cursing a miserable puppy will only add to its problems.

There are always times in a busy household when a puppy is in the way and rather than shutting it in a room which it may damage out of boredom, a small type of lurcher can be kept out of harm's way in an indoor pen, used like a child's playpen so that the animal can see and hear what is going on around it without being a nuisance. It should be provided with a folded blanket to sleep on and a bone or other toy for occupation: if its bed is put in the pen this might provide a foothold which would enable it to scramble out. A pen for a puppy which will grow to whippet-size or a little taller should measure about 90cm (3ft) square with sides about 70cm (28in) high: this will contain it until it reaches the age of twelve to fourteen weeks, by which time it should be more settled in the home and less liable to get under peoples' feet. If there is any possibility of the puppy getting out, a hinged lid should be fitted because a fall at this age could result in a fractured leg.

Ready-made puppy pens can be bought from pet stores and from advertisers in the canine press, or a handyman can make one by constructing four separate wooden frames (plus another for the lid if necessary) and covering them with wire-mesh, such as Weldmesh or Twilweld, of strong gauge and a mesh small enough to prevent a puppy poking its legs through. The separate panels are erected by joining the corners, top and bottom, with hook-and-eye fasteners, and can be stored flat when not in use.

A larger lurcher puppy is best kept in an outdoor kennel, preferably with a run attached. Several manufacturers of portable buildings also make kennels in various designs: I prefer the type which has the sleeping quarters and the run under one extended roof because this prevents the occupant from sitting out in the rain to become soaked and chilled, as it may if it is anxiously waiting for someone to release it. Again, an outdoor kennel should be used only when there is nobody available to supervise the puppy and not as a day-long prison which will dull the wits of the most intelligent dog. An alternative to a kennel is a horse loose-box or shed of similar design, where the top half-door can be left open to admit sunlight and fresh air and is replaced by a mesh panel to prevent jumping out. Any form of outdoor kennel must be draught and weather proof, and a raised bench is essential so that a puppy or dog does not lie on cold concrete – even though this may be well bedded.

There are three kinds of bedding suitable for an outdoor kennel: only wheat straw should be used because the awns on the heads of barley straw irritate the skin and oat straw is too hard; wood-wool makes a warm bed but is apt to be tangly until it is broken down in use; and I now prefer shredded paper which can be bought in bales from stockists who supply it for stables as well as kennels. Paper is clean and warm and makes a good springy bed, provided that is renewed at frequent intervals.

Any form of bedding must be kept clean if the dog is to remain clean, because excess oil in the coat is transferred to the bedding where it becomes rancid grease which is picked up on the hair to give the animal an unpleasant 'doggy' smell and a dull, dusty coat beloved by skin parasites. This applies usually to blankets used in indoor dog beds which should be washed and thoroughly dried and aired every week. Dogs kept on clean bedding seldom, if ever, need to be bathed.

A puppy should have its own food bowl which is washed after each meal, and a bowl kept permanently filled with clean fresh water in a readily accessible place so that it is always able to quench its thirst. A clear Pyrex or similar pudding basin makes a good food bowl because it can be seen to be clean after washing; a glazed pottery dog dish with a lipped edge is better for water as it cannot be tipped over.

Worming and inoculation

A puppy should be treated against roundworms as a matter of routine. A respectable breeder will have dosed it at about six weeks old, but this has to be checked when collecting a new puppy as it will need dosing again at from three weeks to a month later. Puppies under six months old are unlikely to suffer from tapeworms but if these parasites are suspected treatment should be given only under veterinary advice because a proprietory vermifuge could be too strong for a puppy's delicate inside. Worms and worming are dealt with in detail in Chapter Ten.

It is vital to inoculate with a combined vaccine covering distemper, hard-pad, hepatitis and leptospiral jaundice. This should be done a clear month after a puppy has been finally weaned from its dam's milk – otherwise antibodies obtained from her could cancel the effect of the inoculation. Whether it is necessary to give further protection by inoculating against canine parvovirus should be discussed with a vet: it is probably unnecessary for a dog used solely for sport locally but if it is to travel and meet strange dogs from other areas, the extra expense may be worthwhile on the principle of being safe rather than sorry. Booster inoculations are needed for all these vaccines, usually at yearly intervals, and the vet should be asked about these.

Adult dogs running on pasture frequented by sheep and rabbits are almost certain to become infested with tapeworms now and again, and so it is as well to dose them every six months or so to keep them clear.

Grooming

Dogs, like horses, benefit from grooming which not only clears the coat of dust, scurf and the eggs of parasites, but also helps to activate the sebaceous glands in the hair roots to give a gloss and tone up the skin and underlying muscles. I use horse brushes on my dogs: a dandy for wiry hair and a body brush for smooth coats, and find them better than purpose-made dog brushes which are ususally too small to hold comfortably in the hand. A very dirty dog can be cleaned by using a chalk block or powder, rubbed into the coat 'against the grain' and then brushed out, but since this tends to remove natural oil as well it should not be overdone. A large sponge of the type used to wash cars is an asset to a grooming kit: it can be soaked in warm water (and a dog shampoo if necessary) and wiped over parts of the coat which are really clogged with mud, cow dung or whatever muck a dog may have stumbled into, and then squeezed out and recharged with clean water to rinse. This is much better than giving an animal an all-over bathing, particularly in cold weather when there is a risk of chilling.

A wet dog, whether this is due to washing or to exercise in the rain, should always be given a brisk rub down with a rough towel and must not be allowed to sit about shivering in a draught, because this is the best way to lay the foundations of later rheumatism and arthritis which can knock years off the expected life-span of an otherwise healthy dog. With this in mind, a towel should be taken if it is to travel by car to some sporting event.

Honey. A fawn bitch of Smithfield descent. The bold, round eyes and broad skull are guides to potential intelligence, and the hindquarters are obviously spring-loaded for speed, but a greater depth of chest might improve her staying ability.

Lurchers should have their toe-nails trimmed short, which will make the nails less liable to break. If this treatment is given regularly from early puppyhood a dog soon learns to accept the clippers, whereas in later life it may violently resent any attempts to cut its nails: largely out of fear because the quick is as sensitive as our own and an ill-judged clip can be very painful. The quick shows pink in a light-coloured nail but, unfortunately, the majority of lurchers have dark ones which need great care if they are to be cut at the correct length, which can be judged by looking on the underside where a slight groove shows toward the unfeeling tip, but it is better to take off too little rather than risk hurting the dog – which will remember and for ever after be difficult about accepting a manicure. Many people advise clipping at a slant but I have found it better to cut the nail square: after a little exercise on hard ground this will wear to a normal angle, making the nail shorter than one would dare to clip.

Clothing

While accepting that the lurcher is, or should be, a tough animal which ought not to be pampered, there are times when a custom-made rug is a comfort when a dog has to stand about on a cold, blustery day, perhaps waiting to take part in some event. This applies particularly to dogs which have inherited a fine-textured coat from greyhound forbears. There are three main types of rug: wool, macintosh, and, recently, a padded rug in the same material as an anorak which combines the virtues of the other two.

Exercise

Once a puppy has reached the age of six months it can begin exercising on a lead beyond the confines of home territory; short distances at first, progressing gradually so that by eight months it is walking a total of two miles there and back and at a year is covering up to double or treble that distance, depending on the energy of its owner. Walking road work is quite different to galloping in a paddock, building shoulder muscles and muscles on the thigh and second thigh of the hind legs, and generally toning up the whole body. A spell of free exercise in a suitable field should be allowed before turning for home but beware of steep places where a

Star. Bred from greyhound/deerhound X greyhound/sheepdog parentage, he is a most attractive blue and white dog, but a tendency to stray within reach of a motorway forced his owners to have him gelded and this has ruined his figure. Neutering both dogs and bitches almost always has an unavoidable fattening effect, and so this kind of surgery should be looked upon as a last resort.

gangling puppy may trip head over heels and hurt itself (I have seen a terrier of mine, in pursuit of a rabbit, tumble some thirty metres down a hill transversed by sheep paths: a fall like this would have done a lurcher no good at all, whereas a compact Jack Russell merely rolled in a bundle and then went on after its quarry).

A muscular yearling lurcher can be allowed to course a few rabbits now and again but, in my opinion, the majority are not mature enough to tackle anything bigger until they are approaching two years old. This restraint will pay off in the long run, because too much exercise too early is risking heart strain in a dog which has only just started its sporting career.

The working day

The natural sequence of events for a predator is to find, hunt, kill and then eat its prey: replete it returns to its lair to sleep and digest until renewed hunger urges another foray. A lurcher, on the other hand, is expected to hunt and burn up a great deal of energy on a working day, and yet wait until the evening before being fed and allowed to sleep. All hunting dogs, whether they be foxhounds or lurchers, go out 'sharp set' after a light meal the previous evening because a full stomach would both slow them down and blunt their keenness, but with the prospect of a hard day I have made a practice of giving my dogs the benefit of a raw egg before starting out: this puts no strain on the system while providing some extra nourishment for a dog which is going to take a vast amount of exercise within a comparatively short space of time.

If a whole day is spent coursing a dog should be given a rub down when there is a pause for lunch; this will not only partially dry a wet coat but also relieve stretched muscles. The dog will probably need a drink: water in most cases, although a lot of dogs enjoy warm, well-sugared tea or coffee and my old part-whippet, Tip, always looked for a small tot of whisky in hers – in fact, roughly a teaspoonful. Water should be taken in a bottle unless there is a handy stream where a dog can drink: puddles on arable farmland nowadays are suspect because agricultural chemicals can leach into them and perhaps poison a thirsty dog.

On returning home in the evening a tired dog should have priority: it needs a warm feed before it retires to its bed or stretches out on the hearth rug to sleep. Next morning the coat can be brushed to remove dried mud and it is worth running a hand over the skin to find any embedded thorns before these cause inflammation.

Discipline

Anyone who keeps several dogs will know that a top dog emerges in a group to whom the rest are more or less subservient. This dog (or bitch) keeps control without resorting to a fight by force of character and an occasional firm reminder, when it will take a young culprit by the scruff and give it a shake and a growl of disapproval. I work on the same principle in disciplining my dogs, after having made certain that without a shadow of doubt the animal was consciously disobedient and knows the reason for the scolding. Never berate a dog out of temper but act coldly; hold it below each ear, stare into its eyes (which it will hate) and make growly *ugh* sounds. This is far more effective than any amount of lambasting, which

A beautiful head set on a long but powerful neck, with plenty of room for brains, a kind eye and strong jaws.

could injure a dog and cow its spirit.

An affectionate companion lurcher which has been subjected to the wrath of its own personal god is an utterly forlorn animal and one that should be forgiven before too long: active forgiveness is better than letting a dog cringe back to a normal relationship, hoping that the crime is forgotten. As an example, when I was young my parents' household included six Jack Russell terriers: a rumbustious mob which took some managing but my mother had established an extraordinary rapport with them which allowed her to say to a trouble-maker, 'Leave the room!', whereupon a small dog would crouch its way out into the hall and then return to peer anxiously round the drawing-room door. No notice was taken of it for a while and then it was told, 'Come and be forgiven', and it would burst into the room in a flurry of joy. This form of discipline worked perfectly apart from a problem with onlookers who were apt to collapse with laughter and spoil the stern atmosphere.

The elderly lurcher

Man has bemoaned the short life span of a dog since civilisation began, but the owner of a greyhound type is luckier than some in that the majority of long-dog breeds have better prospects of longevity than dogs that have been bred with an unnatural conformation. However, this presupposes extra care as the years go by. A dog qualifies for a veteran class in a show after the age of seven, but a lurcher which has been properly looked after throughout its life should live at least twice as long as this in good condition.

As a rule, seven is too early to begin geriatric treatment but by the time a dog is ten years old it will be slowing down and in need of somewhat different management. It will benefit from reverting to two meals a day, so that the stomach is not overloaded, and the food should be easily digestible as well as nourishing, with plenty of milk, meat and eggs. Beef shin bones will keep the teeth clean and help digestion.

Exercise should be gradually reduced and violent activity, such as jumping gates, avoided, but, at the same time, the dog must be allowed to enjoy itself and have an opportunity of an hour's rabbiting on fine days. Given a chance, an old dog will show its limits but the very devoted kind must be watched to ensure that they are not attempting too much in a faithful effort to keep up as they did in their youth. If younger dogs are to be taken out coursing, an old one should be left secure, comfortable in its bed with a bone, before the excitement starts, so that it is unaware of what is afoot.

It is a good plan to have an elderly dog checked at about six month intervals by a vet, who will be able to diagnose incipient heart failure or other ills. A dry cough is often the first sign of heart trouble, which can be controlled with pills if it is discovered early enough. Sadly, dogs are as prone as human beings to various forms of malignant tumour and, in most cases, a dog should be put down immediately this is diagnosed – an exception may be mammary tumours in a bitch which can be operable if caught in the early stages.

Kipling bade us to beware 'Of giving your heart to a dog to tear'. Although modern drugs allow a vet to give a simple injection which results in merciful oblivion within less than a second, it is still a traumatic experience to decide that an old companion dog has reached the end of its happy days and to comfort it during its last moments, but I believe that it is a bounden duty to stay with the dog, giving it reassurance as if this were just another inoculation. Afterwards one can weep or get drunk.

7 Training

A PUPPY'S training should be taken in stages rather like a child's progression from infant school through junior school to high school, bearing in mind that the ability to learn varies with each individual and the patience and skill of the instructor is all important. Some puppies are slow learners but once they grasp a lesson it is remembered, while others that appear keen and quick at an early age deteriorate to become naughty and boisterous with the approach of adulthood. Training a dog depends first and foremost on establishing a rapport so that it wants to obey in order to please its owner and prove its intelligence, and on making sure that it fully understands one command before it is asked to learn another and is never allowed to get away with outright conscious disobedience.

Picking up the scent of a fox. A working terrier makes a good ally for a pair of lurchers, bolting quarry from cover for them to course.

Basic lessons

Assuming that a puppy is to live in the house it must learn to be clean and this is done by forstalling its need to relieve itself by putting it outdoors after each feed, when it wakes up from sleep and at intervals while it is active – particularly during play. A young puppy appears to have no warning of a need to urinate, often squatting in mid-stride, but does get some prior message about an impending bowel movement which makes it trot about in an urgent manner and this allows time for it to be taken out. The old fashioned method of rubbing a puppy's nose in an accidental pool achieves nothing beyond frightening it. A dog is instinctively clean if it is given a chance.

Next it must learn its name and respond to it by coming when it is called. The quickest way to achieve this is to say the name each time something nice is going to happen; 'Bonnie, dinner!' is the most welcome but a romp in the garden or just an exchange of affection should be prefixed by 'Bonnie, come!'. Training should always be given on the basis of praise for even the smallest show of obedience, and any blame ought to be restricted to a few shocked comments without using the puppy's name. Children, with the best intentions, can retard training by constantly shouting the puppy's name and encouraging it to wild antics which both bewilders and excites it to riotous behaviour, and they must be told that while a puppy benefits from gentle attention its training is a serious business.

A puppy must be taught to accept the restriction of a collar and lead early in its career. The collar should be of soft light leather and worn loose enough to allow a finger to be inserted; the lead may be of light leather but, at this stage, a length of baler string or clothes line will do as well since the puppy will not be taken beyond the house and garden until it is older and adequately protected against virus disease. It is important that lead training should not begin with a scene reminiscent of playing a hooked marlin and this can be avoided by allowing the lead to trail while the puppy gets used to it, and then picking up the end, keeping it slack and calling to bring the puppy in voluntarily, when it should be met with praise. After a few sessions on these lines the sight of its collar and lead will trigger interest, not apprehension. On the other hand, allowing a panic situation, with the puppy leaping and straining back trying to slip the collar, will not only slow the training process but also risks a wrenched neck. Neither a collar nor a lead should be worn when a puppy is unattended because there is a danger of one or other snagging and the possibility of strangulation.

As a rule a puppy should not be taken on foot outside the garden or an adjoining paddock until it is six months old, but this does not mean it must be isolated from the noise and bustle of the world; in fact this would be a great mistake and so the answer is to take it in the car whenever possible.

Most dogs are keen motorists but an odd one may suffer from car-sickness and this is believed to be due to static electricity in a vehicle insulated by rubber tyres – a theory born out by the fact that a chain trailing from the chassis almost always effects a cure, although occasionally puppies are sick due to nerves, because they have not been given an introduction to this new means of travel but merely shoved into the back of a van and jolted round the neighbourhood at high speed; often partially mesmerised by the light-dark shadows of telegraph poles or trees flashing by and the effort of focusing on a receding landscape, which is unnatural for an animal and, indeed, for humans too – during World War II it was found that troops who were frequently transported in covered trucks with only a rear view commonly suffered some degree of eye-strain.

A puppy acquired at eight weeks old should be quite a sophisticated character by the age of four months: clean, responding eagerly to the call of its name, walking sensibly on a lead and travelling by car as if to the manner born. A slow developer may need more time but, given sympathetic training, the majority should achieve this standard at least.

Early working lessons

I know that many lurcher owners allow their dogs to pursue rabbits and hares, and even foxes, at the age of seven or eight months, but really this is both short-sighted and silly (comparable with entering a three year-old in the Grand National: it might get round but it would never be the same again). A three-quarter grown puppy does not possess the bone, muscle or heart for a testing course over rough ground, with the chance of a fall or a wrenching tussle with a resist-quarry, while over-exertion can leave a permanently weakened heart. Successful greyhound trainers, who are not generally renowned for a sentimental attitude towards dogs, allow their puppies to play in a paddock until the age of eight months, when they begin walking road work to encourage muscular development before going into racing training soon after the age of a year. On the same principle, I suggest that even a yearling lurcher should be restricted to taking easy rabbits, and otherwise is much better employed learning its trade as a crafty catcher of game and working partner to its owner: it has a lot to learn.

A puppy of around four months old can start learning three lessons, all of which involve response to command. These are: 'Sit' or 'Down', 'Fetch', and 'Over' (jump an obstacle). There are two important points to remember about commands: first, the words must sound clearly different to avoid the sort of confusion which can result in using 'Sit!' and 'Seek!' as commands, and, second, bear in mind that a dog's hearing is very acute and parade ground shouting will achieve nothing beyond probably tempting the puppy to switch-off and not listen to a deafening noise;

whereas a voice kept at a level which can just be heard by an attentive dog is much more likely to make it listen and respond.

Teaching a dog to sit or lie down is easy enough with a little gentle persuasion and a lot of patience: everyone knows that you press a puppy's hindquarters until it sits, then say 'Good dog, sit!' and walk slowly backwards until the puppy follows, when it is taken back to the same spot and the whole thing starts all over again. Eventually, it will remain sitting (or lying down) while the trainer reverses for several metres and then walks past and round it and away out of sight if that is thought necessary. Once the idea of staying put has been thoroughly instilled, a puppy can be recalled from a distance by the command 'come!' followed by a high-pitched whistle – one brief note by anyone able to whistle, preferably through the teeth, or in a short blast on a mechanical whistle. An obedient response should be congratulated before the puppy is made to sit at the trainer's side. Using two forms of command, word and whistle, for one action means that either can be employed in the field where a whistle does not alert a wild animal which would flee at the sound of a human voice.

If at between four and five months a puppy has learned to sit and stay sitting until recalled, it is doing very well, and if it fails to reach this stage so early keep on patiently working until 'the penny drops', but, at all costs, avoid over-taxing and boring a slow learner as this is often the best way to make a promising animal into a sullen delinquent. While lessons are kept at a friendly level with the puppy earning praise for obedience there is no need for actual prizes, but if training seems to have got into the doldrums and both man and dog are bored by a lack of progress, then a titbit prize can restore flagging spirits. The prize should be small – something to taste and swallow all in a moment, such as a chocolate drop or a morsel of cheese; it is a mistake to give biscuits as these bring lessons to a halt while the puppy chomps the biscuit and then searches for crumbs. Prizes in kind should be phased out as soon as work is once more going ahead satisfactorily, being replaced by hearty praise and the odd titbit now and again at the end of a session.

However adept a lurcher may become at killing game it is not of much use if it stands over the dead quarry, or worse worries the animal to a rag, instead of retrieving a clean kill – this, of course, applies to hares and rabbits; it will have to remain with a fox or small deer. Retrieving, therefore, is an important part of the training programme, which should be begun as soon as possible. No puppy which is going to be expected to retrieve should be allowed to play with a ball, rubber ring or stick as these toys encourage chewing, and, obviously, a game involving a tug of war will do infinite harm. The only object a puppy should be allowed to hold in its teeth (apart from a bone) is a soft dummy, either in the form of a stuffed rabbit skin or an old sock crammed with other old socks, and then only while learning to retrieve.

Waiting for orders after picking up and retrieving a rabbit. It is vital that lurchers are trained to follow instructions when they are running on farmland. Most farmers will allow ground game rights to the owner of a lurcher which is seen to be obedient and safe with domestic livestock.

The first stage in this lesson is to hold the puppy with one hand and chuck the dummy a short distance with the other, making sure that it lands in full view. Then release the puppy, giving the command 'Fetch!'; assuming that it responds, call it in at the moment it picks up the dummy, using a warm voice to welcome it back and, if necessary, exchanging the dummy for a small titbit if the puppy shows any unwillingness to part with the trophy. This initial lesson can be learned in the sitting-room or on the lawn: always as fun and not overdone so that it becomes boring, when a puppy may think it more amusing to make off with the dummy and turn the lesson into a game of tag. If this happens stop the lesson and start again next day with more care.

A gundog is required to retrieve to hand because its handler is encumbered with a gun and does not want to bend down to pick up game dropped at his feet, but this is not important for someone working a coursing lurcher, although retrieving to hand is more stylish. The essential is that the dog brings its kill and does the minimum of damage to the carcass – no lurcher can be expected to have the soft mouth of a spaniel or retriever, but careful teaching with a soft dummy will go a long way towards gentling its jaws.

When the puppy is eagerly retrieving a dummy from a seen fall, it can advance to the stage of finding one tossed into undergrowth or tall grass, and progress to seeking previously hidden dummies, responding to 'fetch!' and gestures from the handler. At all stages the lessons must be fun and every successful retrieve greeted with cries of admiration – everyone thrives on praise, not least a puppy.

I have emphasised the importance of making sessions a pleasure for both man and dog while appreciating that this idea may not appeal to the old school who are inclined to breaking rather than training a working dog; using the submissive nature of a dog to enforce discipline. This kind of strict obedience is commonly found in keeper-trained labradors which have had all initiative drilled out of them and as a result often prove useless at shoots other than highly organised events. The essence of a good lurcher (and, indeed, a companion gundog or sheepdog) is an animal capable of using its own intelligence to work with its handler for mutual benefit, and so I defend my attitude to training on the grounds that hunting with the aid of a dog which is putting all its enthusiasm into the chase is far more rewarding than working a sullen animal which, like a circus lion, reacts to orders only for fear of the whip.

Most dogs naturally jump obstacles within their scope and most lurchers are small-scale steeplechasers, but not all are willing to try a five-barred gate unless brought up to recognise their ability to leap. A puppy can start by being encouraged to hop over a board about 25cm (10in) wide, bracketed on either side so that it stands firmly on edge to represent a solid

Hurdling a five-barred gate is no problem for a large lurcher in pursuit of a hare, but asking a dog to jump such a height 'cold' should be restricted as a slip while changing feet at the top can result in a bad fall. This is why some owners will not take part in cross-country tests at shows.

fence. This barrier can be used indoors or out – in conjunction with retrieving lessons; perhaps using the command 'hup!' or some such to indicate 'jump'. Once a puppy has got the idea of jumping it will try greater heights for itself as it grows in stature and physique.

While the ability to jump is essential to a lurcher's work, there are intrinsic dangers in hurdling over gates and fences because agile dogs, in common with National Hunt and show jumping horses, may drop their hind legs in mid-leap with disastrous consequences: the worst example can happen to a dog jumping a stranded wire fence when the hind legs drop between the top and second strands and the hocks catch, catapulting the animal over the fence to hang head downwards held by its pinned hamstrings. It needs little imagination to realise how difficult it is to extricate, single-handed, an animal in this position or how much damage it is likely to have suffered. Happily I have not had this experience with a dog but once, on a solitary walk, found a blackface ram hanging from a fence and had an appalling job releasing him: he took off at a crippled gallop showing bloody hind legs and I could only hope for the best for him.

The average wire cattle fence measures about 120cm (4ft) in height and, in the heat of the chase, a medium or large lurcher will leap this with ease nine times out of ten but I would still try to avoid this happening by working away from a fence whenever possible. However, there are situations in which it is necessary to get a dog on the far side of a fence, perhaps in order to quarter a likely stubble field, and then I have found it invaluable to have trained it from puppyhood to jump over a coat or my sleeved arm laid along the top (I have taught, among others, all my labradors to do this). A puppy will soon learn to jump the outstretched arm of someone sitting on the floor or lawn and progress to jumping a jacket covering an obstacle, and this lesson is remembered when it starts work.

A lurcher puppy which is to become an all-round sporting companion should be accustomed to the sound of gunfire from an early age – some collies are pitifully gun-shy due, I believe, to their hyper-acute sense of hearing, and this tendency can be passed on to lurcher descendants if these are not given sympathetic training to a gun when they are young. Since cartridges are so expensive, my puppies were initially introduced to gunfire by using blown-up paper bags, which can be burst to make a noise closely resembling the sound of a twelve bore shotgun: this needs two people so that the puppy can be held on a lead by its owner while an accomplished bag-burster stands about the length of a tennis court away. The puppy should be on a lead so that it cannot run away if it is startled, but in most cases it will accept the sudden loud noise if it is reassured by a hand on its scruff and given a lot of warm-voiced encouragement, suggesting excitement and fun ... 'Watch now, good dog, look!' ... until it is keyed-up and staring in the right direction when the 'gun' is signalled.

A related trio. The greyhound/sheepdog dam in the centre is flanked by two of her offspring from one litter sired by a deerhound/greyhound dog. Unpredictable results make lurcher breeding all the more interesting and complicated.

Immediately the explosion has sounded and as the puppy naturally begins to flinch it must be forestalled by being told what a good clever dog it is, which turns its mind from fear to pleasure. The explosions should be restricted to about two on the first day and then, always avoiding fright, the bursts can come progressively nearer until the puppy will remain unconcerned when a bag is exploded almost beside it. If this lesson is learned at the age of ten to twelve weeks few, if any, puppies will be gun-shy in later life even if they never again hear a gun until they are out working in the field.

By the time it is six or seven months old a puppy which has undergone this series of lessons should sit on command and come to recall, responding both to voice and whistle; retrieve seen and hidden dummies and to some extent answer to hand signals; it will leap limited obstacles (not high enough to risk strains) and jump over an arm or coat on command, and it will be accustomed to gunfire; and above all it will take pride in doing all this. It can now begin road work, going for walks on a lead to build muscles and meet the outside world at first hand.

One of the things it will meet is farm livestock and it *must* learn to be absolutely steady with all forms of domestic animal, including poultry; all the more so because it is a lurcher and therefore a dog with a doubtful reputation as far as farmers and landowners are concerned. I think the best way to meet this problem is to ask for the help of a neighbouring farmer, so that a puppy can be taken on a lead to watch when sheep are gathered for shearing, dipping or other attention, when they will be milling about and creating enough noise and smell to slightly alarm a puppy and, at the same time, accustom it to these creatures so that they cease to be objects of wonder or interest. Regular visits to a market can have the same effect. If a puppy makes any attempt to strain on its lead towards the animals it should be given a sharp tug and told 'NO!' in a voice that really means it. Owners of part saluki or slughi (or, heaven forbid, Afghan) lurchers must take particular care because the behaviour of sheep is similar enough to that of antelope as to make them highly attractive prey to dogs of this breeding. It should be noted that English law has recently changed to make it an offence to exercise a dog in a field containing farm livestock, regardless of whether the dog chases them or not.

Advanced lessons

A young lurcher destined to take part in various forms of hunting and in coursing events needs to know about quartering a field from a 'send away'; about working with a lamp at night; about ferrets and ferreting to bolt rabbits; and it must learn to meet and respect other dogs, when necessary working with another to course a hare without becoming aggressive towards its hitherto unknown partner, even though it is an adversary in competitive coursing.

Quartering can be done in two ways: going ahead of the handler, traversing the field to and fro until a rabbit or hare is put up and coursed; or by going away round the perimeter of the field before quartering back towards the handler, or more likely a long net, driving ground game as if the lurcher was a sheepdog gathering a flock. Quartering ahead is reasonably easy to teach by means of 'planted' dummies put out, without the dog's knowledge, at about fifty metre intervals right and left across a paddock. A puppy which has learned retrieving with the aid of an arm pointing right or left will soon get the idea, picking up and retrieving one dummy after another while it criss-crosses the ground; sending away to work backwards to the handler is a more difficult lesson unless the puppy is blessed with at least twenty five per cent trial-bred collie parentage, when it may do this instinctively in response to arm gestures. Otherwise explaining what is required will probably need the help of two people, one at the extreme right or left and the other straight ahead at the far side of the paddock: the handler then gestures the puppy away while the first helper calls it and then gestures to the second (each in turn encouraging the puppy), so that it ends up facing its handler who should not call but wave right and left to start it quartering in search of dummies, which in this case have not been laid if the object of the exercise is to drive, rather than

A greyhound/Irish wolfhound bitch which has inherited the drop-ears of her wolfhound dam. Although wolfhounds are popular in Australia and the USA for breeding the types of lurchers known respectively as kangaroo hounds and coyote hounds, they are seldom used in England where the usual quarry is smaller.

course, game into a net. To my mind, driving is not a fit occupation for a good coursing lurcher and I am not surprised that even the most intelligent puppy often needs weeks of patient instruction before it grasps what it is supposed to do. A simpler way of working to a long-net is to lay the trap and then walk round the field with the puppy to set it off quartering ahead towards the net, while one handler follows at a discreet distance to pick up the catch.

While dummies are an essential part of training, there comes a time when a young dog is liable to become bored if it is everlastingly asked to find and retrieve nothing else, and, before this happens, when the puppy is say eight or nine months old, it is a good idea to let it catch and kill an easy rabbit in order to whet its appetite for hunting. This first kill must be carefully stage-managed to insure success because there is nothing more disheartening for a dog than to put up one rabbit after another and see them all disappear down burrows. Rabbits are likely to be tempted further away from sanctuary on a warm midsummer evening as the light begins to fade and this is when a handler, with stealth, can place the puppy between them and their burrows before releasing it from a slip to mark and catch one – and let it be only one to begin with, which the puppy should retrieve and be met with congratulations before returning home; allowing a killing spree in the first instance can over-excite a puppy and spoil its training.

Picking up somewhat
clumsily done by an
inexperienced bitch.

A good retrieve of an undamaged rabbit.

This puppy with his first rabbit is uncertain what to do next and must learn to retrieve before he can become a useful worker.

Once given an occasional opportunity to kill, I like a puppy to learn that a sibilant breath means 'be alert, watch!'; it quickly understands the hissing sounds and wild animals take no notice of it. Equally, it is now time to discard vocal commands in favour of gestures and a short high-pitched whistle in place of 'come!'. The work will be silent in future.

Lamping is good sport and an excellent way of providing for the larder if a dog has been properly trained to work with a lamp, hunting and picking up only within the beam: a dog that runs riot in the dark alerts hares and rabbits in all directions and risks injury by colliding with unseen hazards. The best way to teach this is to choose a dark night and to work in a paddock or on other ground known to be free of game, using placed dummies which can be brought to light with the lamp and retrieved in the usual manner. If the puppy strays beyond or to either side of the beam it must be whistled in and then started again, so that it understands that it must keep within the lit area. It will need several sessions to perfect this new work but once learned it should be ready to be taken to a spot likely to produce another easy rabbit mesmerised by the lamp, and, such is the intelligence of the average lurcher, it will quickly appreciate the advantages of keeping to the light.

A lurcher which is to work with ferrets should be introduced at an early age to a trustworthily tame ferret, accustomed to dogs and so unlikely to fasten its teeth into an innocently inquisitive nose. A puppy soon recognises the characteristic smell of a ferret and learns to accept it as it does the family cat.

The new owner of a lurcher will quickly realise that a good looking puppy attracts an ever-widening circle of friends with the same interest: being waylaid by strangers eager to know how the puppy was bred and offering invitations to meet their own dogs. Once a puppy is safely immunised against virus disease it should be allowed to meet as many other dogs as possible, preferably of its own kind, so that when the time comes for it to work with others it will be neither aggressive nor timid in the presence of strange dogs. If it is to take part in competitive courses, a friend can be asked to couple it with a quiet reliable dog and walk the two about together, so that the puppy becomes accustomed to going 'in harness' with a stranger and to being handled by someone other than its owner. This experience will stand it in good stead when it goes to meets.

Attending any country function where dogs are allowed, including point-to-points, sports fairs, agricultural shows and even a garden fête, will get it used to crowds and noise so that it gains enough confidence to become the ideal companion dog, which can be relied upon to behave with composure in any situation.

8 The Lurcher in Sport

THE Greek general Xenophon writing in the third century BC, laid down certain rules which should govern hare coursing, the most important of these being a fair start for the quarry to insure that a sport did not deteriorate into mere butchery. The hare appears to have been admired since time immemorial: some five hundred years after Xenophon, Arrian wrote, 'I have struck my head with sorrow that the dog had killed so good an antagonist'; while Early Britons considered it a magical animal (leaving us the legacy of a lucky hare's or rabbit's foot) and it was not until the arrival of the Romans that a hare was killed in England.

I must admit to a liking for hares; yet I enjoy seeing one properly coursed with a chance of escape – which, after all, is the essence of sport as opposed to hunting for the pot. It is a regrettable fact that the ownership of a lurcher leads some people to ravage the countryside and even take to poaching, and this can do nothing but harm to the prestige of these dogs. With this in mind, I have tried to suggest a code of behaviour which should be applied while working a lurcher.

Hare coursing

There are three species of native hare in the British Isles: the brown hare (*Lepus europeus*); the mountain hare of the Scottish Highlands (*L. timidus scoticus*) and the Irish hare (*L. hibernicus*). The brown hare is widely distributed in England and is commonly found on flatlands, downs and moors, which gives the coursing enthusiast a variety of terrain on which to try a lurcher; this is a large species and, in my opinion, should not be coursed by part-bred whippets if it is a heavy adult because dogs of their size are only capable of tackling a three quarters grown leveret.

The mountain hare is a smaller animal which moults in winter to change its coat colour from greyish blue to near white. Although considered a Scottish species it is also found on high ground in the northern counties of England and in the Isle of Man; in common with other hares, it prefers to run uphill and only a sturdy lurcher, preferably with some deerhound blood, is able to turn it.

The Irish hare is also a variable species, brown in summer but moulting out white patches in cold conditions. It is slightly bigger than its Scottish relative and has the unusual habit of going to ground when hard pressed, taking refuge under exposed tree roots and similar hidden places. Coursing in the south west of Ireland is more a religion than a sport and it has been said that you may get away with shooting your neighbour but shooting a hare is unforgivable.

There is no close season for hares, except that in most parts of Britain the taking of hares and rabbits is forbidden on Sundays and Christmas Day, but the Ground Game Act (although now seldom invoked) is a complicated law when applied to a tenant farmer, who, technically, is not allowed to permit more than one person to take ground game and that person must carry with him written permission. While this law is unlikely to be a problem, it is as well to be aware of it and to establish and maintain good relations with farmers and landowners. A landowner can invite anyone he chooses to course hares and rabbits provided that shooting rights have not been leased to a third party, when a separate agreement is necessary. All this may seem academic but it is astonishing how many people settle as strangers in a rural community and, much to their surprise, fall foul of farmers when they wander over private land and poach game if an opportunity occurs, little realising that everything in the countryside belongs to somebody. On the other hand, a courteous approach to a farmer, maybe a drink at the pub, and proof beyond doubt that the lurcher in question is obedient and trained to ignore farm livestock can usually allay a countryman's inborn suspicion of these dogs with a somewhat murky past, and arrive at a friendly agreement.

Unlike competitive coursing, the prime objective of coursing on home ground is to kill hares – unless the dog is being trained for competitions – but it is still only ethical to give the quarry a fair start and this means walking over likely ground with the dog held in a slip. A dog which is allowed to range at will either picks up a hare still squatting in its form, or fails to see a hare running at an angle beyond its line of sight. Apart from this it may be distracted by rabbits or find a newborn deer fawn hidden in undergrowth.

A custom-made slip lead is a complicated device and unnecessary for home use when a strip of leather looped round the dog's neck and held at either end will serve just as well: one end is dropped to release the dog, taking care to pull the slip to one side so as to avoid tripping. Do not use a line or baler-string as this can 'burn' a lurcher's skin if it is pulled under tension while slipping, but a cloth, such as a scarf, works reasonably well.

A good coursing lurcher is a crafty dog, not as fast as a greyhound but making up for its lack of speed by using intelligence to judge which way a hare will jink and so pick it up on the turn. The purist accustomed to watching greyhounds coursing may not approve of the lurcher's method but it is none the less highly efficient.

In the eighteenth century coursing was commonly followed on horseback. The first known organised meet took place in 1776 when the Swaffham Coursing Club was founded in East Anglia at a time when that eccentric sportsman Lord Orford was experimenting in cross-breeding greyhounds and lurchers to produce better hunting dogs. Some eighty years later the National Coursing Club came into being and Rules were formulated.

What may be described as 'rough' coursing (since it compares with rough shooting in that it involves walking over a stretch of country looking for quarry, either alone or with one or two friends), is a disorganized sport and for this reason a lurcher is more liable to come up against various hazards, of which barbed-wire can be one of the most damaging. Many accidents could be prevented with a little forethought: for example, walking up a stubble field towards a distant fence may be asking for trouble because a running hare can easily nip under the wire strands whereas a lurcher hell-bent in pursuit may crash against the fence to lacerate itself or even break its neck. In this case it might have been possible to approach the field from a different direction so that the hare is put up with the prospect of a hedge as its salvation. The same precautions apply to ground near stone quarries, railway embankments or highways: it is a matter for that valuable asset, common sense, which sometimes flies out of the window in the heat of the chase.

Competitive coursing

In order to compete successfully at a coursing meet a lurcher must be well

trained and steady but keen; knowing what it is supposed to do and doing it with artistry and dash. It also needs to be good tempered because any signs of aggression will put it out of the running. Unfortunately, many breeders of splendid-looking lurchers fail to take temperament into account and some even more foolish people actively encourage a fighting tendency in their dogs in the belief that an aggressive nature will make them better at catching foxes. A puppy bought from this kind of stock is liable to be worse than useless as a contender in competitive coursing, although sensible handling from an early age can improve its nature in a few cases.

Coursing is a sport which needs to be seen to be understood. In essence it is two dogs working in unison to score individual points which are totalled by a judge who declares one or other the winner. Contrary to the opinion of anti-blood sports supporters killing the hare is incidental, and official figures state that only ten per cent of hares are killed during a greyhound coursing meet, although I suspect that the percentage may be higher when lurchers compete. As for the hare, it must endure considerable fright before it can make its escape through a hedge to freedom, but, such is the speed of the participants, a course is over in a matter of minutes and it is up to the individual onlooker to decide whether watching the expertise of the coursing dogs justifies inflicting a definite, if small, amount of cruelty on the hare. However, I must add that a few disreputable unofficial meets do occur in some parts of the British Isles where escaped hares are netted and returned to run again and again for a succession of dogs, and clearly this practice is extremely cruel and denegrates the sport as a whole.

An official coursing meet is run on the principle of a tournament: winners are matched against winners until one remains as champion of the day. Each dog of a pair is given either a red or a white collar, and they are released from double slips when a hare driven past them has a lead of some sixty to eighty metres. It is at this moment that scoring begins with the dog which first comes up with the hare to gain up to three points, or the dog which starts a clear length behind its opponent and reaches the hare a clear length in front which can count as much; these manoeuvres are known as the *Run-Up* and a *Go-Bye* respectively, and represent the potentially highest points. There remains a *Turn* when a dog forces the hare to turn at more than ninety degrees; a *Wrench* which is the same but the hare turns for less than ninety degrees; a *Kill* (self-explanatory), and lastly, a *Trip* when the hare is toppled or grazed but not held by a dog. The judge from the vantage of horseback oversees the action and signals his decision by means of a red or white flag.

Clearly, an efficient slipper able to release the two dogs without advantage being given to either is essential to a course, but it is up to the owner to train a lurcher to walk and generally behave sensibly on a double slip accompanied by an unknown dog; alert to what is afoot and ready to go on the instant.

A slip, single or double, consists of a lead joined to a collar or collars which is equipped with a release mechanism that opens the throat of the collar to free a single dog or two dogs simultaneously. To expect a novice dog to accept all this without previous training is to expect a miracle.

It is thought by many people who should know that meets held under National Coursing Club rules, and any other public meets, may be banned within a few years in response to constant lobbying by those who disapprove of field sports in general and coursing in particular. In my view this is a pity: it has always been a gentlemanly sport and bears no comparison with other banned pursuits such as badger-baiting and dog fighting, both of which were very nasty indeed.

Netting

A lurcher owner out to catch the maximum number of hares and rabbits, rather than watch the dog pit its wits against those of its quarry, may resort to nets which are undoubtedly efficient but not, I think, to be judged as sporting. In this case the dog is trained to circle the chosen field and then quarter it back and forth in much the same manner as a pointer or setter,

Twigs. A greyhound/whippet X saluki. A cross of this kind produces a dog with a remarkable turn of speed but some individuals may lack the intelligence which is the keynote of a good lurcher.

'shepherding' any ground game towards an open gateway, or a hedge gap, across which a net has been laid. The net is propped, not tied, in place and falls to entangle an animal that runs into it, when the hitherto hidden human members of the party reappear to despatch the catch and move on. Admittedly, a dog must be highly trained to carry out this job but that is all I can say for it.

Lamping

Hares and rabbits can be taken at night by using the lights of an unloved motor car (springs and sundry other parts are not improved by jolting round a field), or a Land-Rover, but the best sport is found by walking round with a hand lamp. Powerful torches depending on a dry battery are now available and these will throw a beam of light across a distance of three hundred metres or so – I have used a torch of this type for checking outlying lambing ewes in danger from foxes and have been fascinated by the amount of wildlife it has illuminated in one sweep, including rabbits, badgers and hedgehogs, all on their more or less lawful occasions.

Lamping is great fun and can produce a considerable harvest for the larder if it is carried out properly. To my mind solitary expeditions are the most satisfactory because if more than one person is present there is a temptation to talk and the human voice alerts every wild creature within earshot.

Apart from a lamp, the equipment needed is a well-trained lurcher and a game bag which can be slung like a haversack: one hand is needed for the torch and the other to hold the dog in a slip or, if it is a tall lurcher, a finger hooked through its collar. It is useless to allow the dog to range in the dark as it will merely bolt every animal in the area with little chance of catching anything, while being liable to injure itself on unseen obstacles.

A mild, dark night without frost or heavy dew is likely to offer good sport – the sort of night that Surtees' character reported as, 'Hellish dark and smells of cheese!' when he blundered into a cupboard. Wet or frozen grass deters hares and rabbits from feeding any distance from shelter, and a moonlit landscape tends to put them on the *qui vive*, on the lookout for a fox. A dog in training for lamp work will have learned that a soft hiss from between his handler's teeth means 'be ready', so that it is all set to go along the beam of light if this shines on quarry, but must know to stop where the light dims regardless of whether it has made a kill or not – if it has, then it should retrieve. If a hare or rabbit squeals when it is caught this will warn others of its kind within hearing distance, but may attract a fox, and so if a small lurcher, which is liable to be damaged in a fight with a fox, is being worked it may be wise to make a discreet retreat to some other field. Equally, the handler of a large lurcher who wishes to take a fox may be rewarded after a short wait in the dark: foxes are often deluded into believing a squeal to be the result of a stoat or weasel's handiwork and arrive to filch easy prey.

Fox and deer hunting

Fox hunting, it cannot be described as coursing because lurchers so far outmatch a fox for speed, is a delicate subject: there are few rural areas in England which are not the hunting country of a pack of foxhounds whose officials will not welcome fox killing by lurchers on their ground. However, since many sheep farmers now begin their lambing season in December those who suffer the depredations of foxes amongst their new-born lambs may be glad to invite the owner of a lurcher to catch a few for sport and the value of their skins.

The season from a foxhunting point of view begins in the autumn after the harvest with cub hunting, which has the twofold purpose of distributing, by chasing, the year's crop of cubs away from their birthplace, and showing the young entry of novice hounds what hunting is all about. Hunting proper starts on 1 November and goes on until early April when vixens breed again – most respectable hunts try to prevent hounds hunting a vixen heavy in whelp but this is not always possible. It seems ethical to use the same principles and season when working a lurcher.

The best and often the most amusing way to hunt foxes is with one or two large lurchers, a couple of Jack Russell terriers and, ideally, a beagle. While on cold dull days a fox will sleep away the daylight hours snug inside its earth, sunny weather can tempt it to bask under a bramble patch or similar warm but hidden place and this is when the terriers and beagle come into their own: making enough noise 'to waken the dead and the fox from his lair in the morning'. Meanwhile, the lurchers are held back until a crescendo of noise warns that a fox is about to bolt. How much leeway is given to it depends on the individual handler: if the lurchers are released as soon as it is clear of the underbrush they will bowl it over in an instant, as a fox takes several seconds to get into top gear and make up its mind where to run. This quick finish is probably more humane than allowing a lapse of time followed by a stern chase to an inevitable end, but the disadvantage is that the animal may try to break back into cover and meet the other dogs head-on, to be torn in pieces and leave a useless pelt.

A fox that is not instantly killed can inflict very nasty bites on an attacking lurcher, injuring its face and legs, and so a thin-skinned greyhound type of dog is not as good for the job as a rough-coated lurcher. Anyone out after foxes ought to be prepared with some means of killing the animal in a proper manner: the best weapon is some sort of blackjack, which can be a short stick loaded with lead or a length of metal pipe – either will crush the skull with one aimed blow.

This brings me to a brief digression on the subject of killing wounded game of all kinds. My own views are based on those taught by my father who hunted and fished and was a keen shot with a 'bag' ranging from grouse to the big game of Africa and India: his strict rule was that it is the first duty of a sportsman to kill quickly and cleanly, and an injured creature as soon as is humanly possible – this was taken to the extent that a member of a shooting party who winged a bird was expected to search (for the rest of the day if necessary) until the 'runner' was found. It saddens me to realise that many people today take little account of the suffering to which game birds, animals and even fish are subjected when they are caught.

Deer of various species are hunted with lurchers for sport and for venison. The three original species native to Britain were red, fallow and roe deer, but these have now been joined in the wild by three foreign species which have escaped from parks: these are Japanese sika, Asian muntjac and Chinese water deer; the last two are small and relatively harmless in the countryside as they tend to be solitary rather than herd animals, but the sika is causing some concern because it resembles a lesser version of the British red deer and will interbreed with it and this is thought likely to have a degenerative effect on the indigenous stock.

A pair of deerhound-bred lurchers can bring down red and fallow deer but a handler must be prepared to make the *coup de grace* by some suitable means, which can be a brain-shot taken behind the ear or failing that, a stab to the heart with a knife that is both long and strong enough for the job. The smaller deer lurk in the undergrowth, coming out at night when it is illegal to take them by any method, and so they must be forced to break in the daytime, usually with the help of the ubiquitous Jack Russells.

It is important to know that a game licence is required for deer hunting (except for an owner or occupier on his own land). A local police station will advise on licences and the various restrictions in force either nationally or locally – these have been recently altered or are in the process of alteration so that listing them here would serve no useful purpose.

Ferreting

Working different animals together for a single purpose is always fascinating. The classic example must be a Sheik riding an Arabian stallion, a falcon on his fist and a brace of salukis running alongside: all intent on hunting gazelle. But, literally coming down to earth, ferreting with terriers and lurchers can be almost as entertaining on a more mundane level, although by no means the best way to clear a warren.

Ferrets are domesticated descendents of the wild polecat which is still occasionally seen in wilder parts of Wales but is otherwise now extinct in

Britain; it is native to most parts of Europe and northern Asia; a much bigger animal than the ferret, often measuring more than 70cm (28in) from nose to tail. The domestic working ferret has been tamed for a very long time: contemporary writings suggest that ferrets were kept loose in the houses of Ancient Greece, replacing cats as vermin hunters. Properly handled, a ferret is a charming creature capable of becoming an affectionate pet and learning to live and work amicably with dogs.

There are two kinds available: the fitch or polecat ferret, which is a small version of the wild species in appearance, and the white ferret which is merely an albino example but, for some reason, is often bigger than coloured ferrets. I have found both types equally good for rabbiting and there is nothing to choose between the sexes, except that females (known as bitches or jills) should be allowed to breed if they are to have a reasonable life span – a maiden jill is liable to die of an ovary infection after a year or so because, in common with a female cat, she will ovulate only *after* mating and, left unmated, will tend to accumulate eggs which eventually form suppurating cysts. A male (dog or hob) will be content enough alone if he is given plenty of work or otherwise carried about in a pocket; his only drawback is that he can rival a billy goat for smell, however clean his hutch is kept.

A dog and a ferret should be introduced under controlled conditions because the dog cannot be blamed for mistaking this strange animal for some kind of rat. Both must be held: the dog by its collar and the ferret by encircling its neck with forefinger and thumb, using the remaining fingers to support its chest, leaving the hind quarters dangling. The ferret is comfortable in this attitude, as long as it is not gripped, and should it become nervous is prevented from turning its head to bite the handler. In talking to the dog I use the term 'No, pet!' but 'Leave!' will do as well. It soon learns to recognise the characteristic smell of a ferret and to accept it as a strange partner and, once reassured, the ferret will do the same. One jill I owned was often allowed indoors in the evening and would gallop about the sitting-room, whistling to herself and being a considerable nuisance to sleeping dogs who tried to pretend that she wasn't there.

Successful ferreting is dependent on finding the right burrows and on silence. An old warren consisting of innumerable intercommunicating passages and bolt holes is not to be recommended: if a ferret is put into a warren of this kind it is likely to trot round chivvying the occupants in all directions until one is cornered and eaten, after which it will lie-up and can be retrieved only after an arduous dig (or the next day when it may be found wandering above ground nearby). Few, if any, rabbits will bolt from a big warren. The ideal site is a series of five or so obviously used entrances in a bank facing an open field where dogs can be placed at strategic points, ready to respond to the command, 'Go!' when one or more rabbits have bolted clear. Avoid a single hole partially blocked with moss and dried grasses as this is almost certainly a doe's nest, and a questing ferret will feast on the hapless young and then again, lie-up or be so satiated as to be useless for the rest of the day.

Silence is essential because the ground acts as a sounding-board and a rabbit hearing the noise of clumping boots is presented with a choice between two evils: stay and face the ferret or bolt into unknown dangers, and most choose to stay; maybe lurking near an entrace but not making a run for supposed safety as they will if there is silence outside.

A couple of terriers are useful for digging-out and most are capable of running down a few bolted rabbits, but this is the true role of the lurcher and excited terriers should not be allowed to get in its way, as this not only spoils its fun but can lead to frayed tempers. All the participants must be properly trained to keep back until told to go by name: this is asking a lot when 'the blood is up' and must be taught from the moment a puppy is capable of learning disciplined behaviour – no sensible rabbit (which have more sense than many people suppose) is going to emerge from its burrow into the jaws of a dog peering in at it, even if the devil himself was at its heels.

A final word on the subject of ferrets: old-fashioned gamekeepers and poachers fed their ferrets on an exclusive diet of bread and milk in the belief that raw meat encouraged killing and lying-up. In fact, the opposite is true because a ferret is a carnivore which naturally desires bloody meat and if it is deprived of this at home it is going to find it down a rabbit burrow. My own ferrets were given chicken heads, young rabbits too small for the table, and damaged parts of larger ones which had been caught by the dogs (plus a constant supply of fresh drinking water), and I had little trouble with underground feasts – a well fed ferret bolts rabbits for sport.

9 Breeding

IT IS tempting to breed from a good bitch, and giving birth and rearing a litter will be beneficial for her, as this natural function helps to mature a female animal both mentally and physically. However, there are various points to consider before embarking on the project: first of all, she will be out of action as far as sport is concerned for a period of about six months (allowing three weeks season, nine weeks gestation, eight weeks with the puppies and, at least, another four weeks to regain working condition); then there is the question of suitable whelping quarters and where the puppies will be penned once they become active, and lastly, a growing litter needs attention throughout the day, which means that somebody reliable must always be at home to look after them. Assuming that all this is acceptable, lurcher breeding is a fascinating hobby.

Choosing a mate

Successful breeding is dependant on matching the right dogs and this is a subject of much controversy in lurcher circles, which can leave a novice bewildered in the midst of a great deal of conflicting advice. In practical terms the bitch's parentage makes a starting point and I will take the two most common crosses first: a deerhound/greyhound should go back to a greyhound and a greyhound/collie to a greyhound or whippet. If the bitch is vaguely described as the offspring of two lurchers, with no further information, then she too is best put back to a greyhound, or, if she is large enough, to a deerhound – in either case the sire should be purebred. A lurcher bitch which is virtually indistinguishable from a greyhound in appearance is not popular and, certainly, ought not to be mated with a greyhound but should visit either a trial-bred collie or a deerhound to produce lurcher-type puppies.

The production of what are considered to be true Norfolk lurchers is quite a complicated process which I will try to clarify: it begins with a cross between a Smithfield collie and a greyhound; the best bitch is chosen from this litter and in due course mated to a greyhound; now a dog puppy is kept and he represents bloodline number one. At the same time (in another part of the forest), a parallel line of unrelated dogs is established by mating a deerhound with a greyhound and keeping a dog from that litter to be bred with a greyhound bitch, and their best bitch puppy is then mated with the dog from bloodline number one to produce a litter of Norfolk's.

This is an old hand's recipe which, obviously, involves keeping and discarding a lot of dogs and that alone makes it beyond the scope of the average owner of a companion bitch, but it can be done without actually owning all the dogs if mates are chosen after careful research into their known ancestory. The two main points to remember are never breed two greyhound types together and choose a puppy which, while built on racy lines, shows more resemblance to its non-greyhound parentage.

That is a twentieth century view of lurcher breeding but going back to the late 1700s the author William Taplin discussing lurchers in his two-volume work *The Sportsmen's Cabinet* (1803) states categorically that a lurcher is bred as a first cross between a shepherd's dog and a greyhound, and thereafter 'in-and-in' to a greyhound. But of course, dogs styled as greyhounds in those days were a mixed bunch: some built on classic lines and others rough haired and more like an undersized deerhound; perhaps more intelligent and biddable than their modern counterparts.

The majority of gypsies with whom I have discussed the subject agree that lurchers should be bred to lurchers, although some like to go back to greyhound and collie crosses now and again, and others include a dash of whippet, Bedlington and terrier. Their criteria is not looks but ability as successful poaching dogs.

It seems, therefore, that it is a case of 'you pays your money and takes your choice', except that it remains important not to produce nondescript mongrels as a result of thoughtless matings between unsuitable dogs.

The saluki and slughi represent alternatives to greyhound parentage and such crosses have proved very useful in competitive coursing, but they do need diluting with collie blood in order to breed intelligent, obedient lurchers.

There is now a trend in favour of small lurchers based on whippet/collie crosses, sometimes with the addition of Bedlington and small greyhound (or large Italian greyhound) blood, as a rule, carefully bred small lurchers are very intelligent and lethal where rabbits are concerned; shows cater for them with under 56cm (22in) classes, but they seldom have much hope when competing in finals against larger dogs.

Quite apart from the most suitable pure and cross-breeds to use, temperament is all-important in a chosen stud dog: he must show himself to be friendly towards humans and dogs, without the least sign of nervousness or aggressive behaviour, because either tendency is likely to be passed on to his progeny, which, however handsome dad may be, will grow up to be a nuisance one way or the other.

The bitch

It is normal practice to mate a bitch during her third season but timing also

Most experienced dog owners prefer to buy a puppy at the age of about eight weeks, but judging its good and bad points can be difficult when it is at this podgy stage. A sloping rather than straight shoulder is important in order to give a running dog scope over the ground.

depends on her age. Bitch puppies usually have their first season when they are about eight months old and then come on again every six months or so, which means that at her third season a bitch is just under two years old and reaching maturity. However, some with strong greyhound influence can delay a first season until they are over twelve months and then it may be better to breed from her in her second. The object is to breed while the pelvic bones are still pliable enough to allow the easy passage of a first litter, but, at the same time, a mentally and physically immature bitch should not be asked to meet the demands of puppies before she is fit for the job.

At this stage I should mention the growing practice of suppressing a bitch's season by means of drugs, which is becoming almost universal for racing greyhounds in order to prevent any hold-up in an often brief career on the track. What concerns many vets is the long-term effect on bitches receiving the drug at every cycle, and this remains to be seen. Meanwhile, I am loath to try the untried on my own valued bitches.

Before she is due in season a bitch intended for mating should be in good hard condition, with plenty of flesh on her bones but not fat; she will need a routine treatment to insure that she is free of tapeworms, and it is a wise precaution to arrange with a vet for a booster inoculation of the comprehensive virus vaccine if this is not up to date, and he will advise on whether an injection against parvovirus is a necessary added protection –

as it will be if this dread disease has recently attacked puppies in the area. All this should be done at least a month before the bitch is due in season so that she is clear of tapeworms and the inoculations will have had time to take effect well in advance of that date.

The ideal time for puppies to be born is in late March so that they are

A hand placed under a puppy's belly to gently lift it will show the depth of chest and conformation of the hind quarters. If it is then allowed to take up a natural stance, the forelegs should be seen to be straight and the hind toes well under the pelvis.

toddling about in April and have the whole summer before them in which to grow and enjoy whatever sunshine the British climate allows. This means that mating should take place at the end of the third week in January but, of course, nature is not always so obliging and all one can plan is to breed in the spring or early summer and avoid breeding in the autumn and winter when puppies would have cold, sunless days and long, dark nights to contend with during their peak growing period.

A bitch begins her season by 'showing colour', passing a few drops of blood; the flow increases during the next eight days or so, and the vulva enlarges and becomes tense until about the tenth day when the issue of blood has decreased and the part softens: at this stage, between the tenth and fourteenth day according to the individual bitch, she will normally be ready to mate. She is likely to be very playful at this time and if she has contact with other bitches will invite them to mount her, turning her tail to the side in invitation. These games have the advantage of exciting her desire to mate but bitches in this highly emotional state should not be left without supervision because what began as a jolly indulgence can end in a serious fight if one of the party loses her temper.

It is the usual practice for the bitch to visit the dog and, if possible, a maiden bitch should go to an experienced dog (and *vice versa*) so that one of the two knows what they are supposed to be doing. Both animals should be held on leads while they sniff each other and make friendly overtures and then may be released together in a well fenced area where they can prance and play: it is important to be sure that the pair cannot escape because dogs are inclined to run off in search of privacy before they mate, and a bitch running with a dog could attract a most undesirable pack of other dogs which might sieze an opportunity to put her in-whelp with a litter of mongrels if the chosen stud lost control of the situation.

Breeders of pedigree dogs usually supervise a mating to the extent of holding the pair but such interference should be unnecessary with lurchers, who may, indeed, resent it and refuse to mate while being handled. Never force a mating by holding a bitch which is not responding to a dog, because she will have good reason for this – perhaps she is not ready or, in rare cases, she instinctively knows that she has some physical defect which prohibits breeding; try her again next day and if she still fails to stand for the dog it will be wise to abandon the project and have her examined by a vet.

Assuming that the bitch does stand and mating takes place, the dogs then 'tie' for a period of up to half an hour or so and must be left until they part naturally, when the bitch should be removed and left quiet in the car for a while before starting for home. A second mating is often arranged within about two days but for dogs in good condition (as they must be), which have mated voluntarily, this is unnecessary nine times out of ten; it really only applies to an overworked stud dog, such as a popular coursing deerhound, greyhound or whippet, which has been in constant demand during the spring season.

The gestation period

There are two important jobs to be done during the initial stages of the gestation period: first, the bitch should be dosed against roundworms within two weeks of mating, because if she was not cleared of these parasites when she was a puppy, they can remain dormant inside her ready to invade her unborn puppies a few days before she gives birth. Not everyone agrees with me but I have found over many years with a variety of breeds that a bitch dosed soon after mating is far less likely to produce a worm-ridden litter.

The second job is to prepare whelping quarters which can be expanded to house the puppies as they grow and become active. A small lurcher bitch can whelp indoors in a bed large enough to allow her to lie full length, her legs outstretched with space to spare, as this will give plenty of room for her and her litter while they are confined to the nest. The bed should be sited in a quiet place away from other animals and household bustle: a scullery or what estate agents describe as a utility room will do if it is reasonably warm but airy. Old carpet cut to fit the bed and overlaid with a piece of clean blanket is sufficient bedding. Some authorities advise fitting dowel-rod bars in the inner sides of a whelping bed as a means of preventing very young puppies from being crushed by the mother when she lies down, but I have never used them because, in my opinion, only a hopeless brood bitch will lie on her puppies – unless too much bedding allows a puppy to creep beneath a blanket or under straw where she is unable to see or feel its presence, which can happen during whelping, with or without bars, when she is occupied by the stress of another birth.

A large lurcher is better outdoors in a dry, draught-proof stable or shed; preferably one wired for electricity to provide light and a point for an infra-red lamp if cold conditions make this necessary. I have converted a loose-box stall as whelping quarters for a large dog by fixing a bed tight to a rear corner and slots on each side wall to take boards which can be built up to retain very young puppies within a restricted floor area during their first ventures from the nest. At a later stage, when they have the freedom of the whole stable, a sheet of chip-board should be fixed across the entrance door to a height of about 70cm (28in), so that an attendant can step over and the bitch can jump in or out, but a mob of puppies are prevented from bursting forth every time the door is opened.

As to the bed, I have made this on the lines of a large packing-case laid on its side, the front open but for a board about 25cm (10in) wide attached to the lower part and hinged so that it can be held upright by sliding slots, to keep the puppies in the nest while they are still helpless, or laid flat on the floor when they become active enough to crawl around. The top of this type of enclosed bed must be high enough to allow the bitch to stand up with head-room to spare. It has a two-fold advantage over an open topped bed in that it is cosier and also provides a shelf refuge for the bitch when her puppies are part-weaned and inclined to be a nuisance to her if she has no means of escape; carpet can be tacked to the top for her comfort.

A bitch with a litter whelped indoors will have to be transferred outside by the time the puppies are about three weeks old unless the room they occupy can be written-off: I made the mistake of making no outdoor provision for the first Italian greyhound litter I bred; keeping them partitioned in a corner of the kitchen on the erroneous assumption that such comparatively tiny puppies would make little mess, but what they achieved in the way of chewed vinyl floor-covering and scratched walls, not to mention copious amounts of solid and fluid excreta, soon taught me a lesson. How much damage a party of baby lurchers may do needs little imagination.

Served Jan	Whelps March	Served Feb	Whelps April	Served March	Whelps May	Served April	Whelps June	Served May	Whelps July	Served June	Whelps Aug.	Served July	Whelps Sept.	Served Aug	Whelps Oct.	Served Sept.	Whelps Nov.	Served Oct.	Whelps Dec.	Served Nov.	Whelps Jan.	Served Dec.	Whelps Feb.
1	5	1	5	1	3	1	3	1	3	1	3	1	2	1	3	1	3	1	3	1	3	1	2
2	6	2	6	2	4	2	4	2	4	2	4	2	3	2	4	2	4	2	4	2	4	2	3
3	7	3	7	3	5	3	5	3	5	3	5	3	4	3	5	3	5	3	5	3	5	3	4
4	8	4	8	4	6	4	6	4	6	4	6	4	5	4	6	4	6	4	6	4	6	4	5
5	9	5	9	5	7	5	7	5	7	5	7	5	6	5	7	5	7	5	7	5	7	5	6
6	10	6	10	6	8	6	8	6	8	6	8	6	7	6	8	6	8	6	8	6	8	6	7
7	11	7	11	7	9	7	9	7	9	7	9	7	8	7	9	7	9	7	9	7	9	7	8
8	12	8	12	8	10	8	10	8	10	8	10	8	9	8	10	8	10	8	10	8	10	8	9
9	13	9	13	9	11	9	11	9	11	9	11	9	10	9	11	9	11	9	11	9	11	9	10
10	14	10	14	10	12	10	12	10	12	10	12	10	11	10	12	10	12	10	12	10	12	10	11
11	15	12	15	11	13	11	13	11	13	11	13	11	12	11	13	11	13	11	13	11	13	11	12
12	16	13	16	12	14	12	14	12	14	12	14	12	13	12	14	12	14	12	14	12	14	12	13
13	17	14	17	13	15	13	15	13	15	13	15	13	14	13	15	13	15	13	15	13	15	13	14
14	18	15	18	14	16	14	16	14	16	14	16	14	15	14	16	14	16	14	16	14	16	14	15
15	19	16	19	15	17	15	17	15	17	15	17	15	16	15	17	15	17	15	17	15	17	15	16
16	20	17	20	16	18	16	18	16	18	16	18	16	17	16	18	16	18	16	18	16	18	16	17
17	21	18	21	17	19	17	19	17	19	17	19	17	18	17	19	17	19	17	19	17	19	17	18
18	22	19	22	18	20	18	20	18	20	18	20	18	19	18	20	18	20	18	20	18	20	18	19
19	23	20	23	19	21	19	21	19	21	19	21	19	20	19	21	19	21	19	21	19	21	19	20
20	24	21	24	20	22	20	22	20	22	20	22	20	21	20	22	20	22	20	22	20	22	20	21
21	25	22	25	21	23	21	23	21	23	21	23	21	22	21	23	21	23	21	23	21	23	21	22
22	26	23	26	22	24	22	24	22	24	22	24	22	23	22	24	22	24	22	24	22	24	22	23
23	27	24	27	23	25	23	25	23	25	23	25	23	24	23	25	23	25	23	25	23	25	23	24
24	28	25	28	24	26	24	26	24	26	24	26	24	25	24	26	24	26	24	26	24	26	24	25
25	29	26	29	25	27	25	27	25	27	25	27	25	26	25	27	25	27	25	27	25	27	25	26
26	30	27	30	26	28	26	28	26	28	26	28	26	27	26	28	26	28	26	28	26	28	26	27
27	31	28	1	27	29	27	29	27	29	27	29	27	28	27	29	27	29	27	29	27	29	27	28
28	1	29	2	28	30	28	30	28	30	28	30	28	29	28	30	28	30	28	30	28	30	28	1
29	2			29	31	29	1	29	31	29	31	29	30	29	31	29	1	29	31	29	31	29	2
30	3			30	1	30	2	30	1	30	1	30	1	30	1	30	2	30	1	30	1	30	3
31	4			31	2			31	2			31	2	31	2			31	2			31	4

The gestation period for a bitch is nine weeks, or, more exactly, averages sixty-three days; puppies born before the sixtieth day rarely survive and if a bitch goes beyond the sixty-fifth day she should be checked by a vet who can use a stethoscope to hear if the puppies are still alive – always remembering that if a second mating took place a day or two after the first, it may have been the fertile one.

From the mating date onwards a bitch should be given extra vitamins and minerals, and a nourishing diet provided by meat, eggs and milk, plus green vegetables and best quality wholemeal biscuit. The additives required are calcium and phosphate and cod-liver oil to give vitamins A and D, which respectively promote growth in the young animal and, combined with calcium, assist the formation of strong bones. Without these extras a bitch carrying a large litter may draw on her own reserves and perhaps suffer from milk fever soon after the puppies are born. Additives must be given strictly according to the maker's instructions.

In the course of the first five weeks of pregnancy a bitch can lead a normal life, but should not be allowed to take exhausting exercise, or jump. After that time most will show that they are in-whelp and become progressively heavier. Those normally on one or two meals a day should have these reduced in size and increased in number, because when the puppies begin to take up more and more room inside her the bitch is unable to eat a large meal.

A week before the expected birth date she should be shown the whelping quarters which have been arranged for her and encouraged to enter the bed every day, because as her time approaches she will be uneasy if there is no obvious place where she can retire. Some bitches revert to primitive instinct, moving round and round in the bed, attempting to tear up the blanket to make a nest, and she can be given shredded paper or soft hay as a temporary substitute.

The birth

In common with other animals, the majority of bitches whelp at night, but she is likely to show signs the previous evening: the teats will be large and droplets of milk can be expressed by gentle pressure; there will probably be a slight discharge of thin, clear mucus, and she will be restless and inclined to lick herself.

She should be put out to empty her bladder and, if she will, the bowels, and then taken to her bed. While a lurcher, with its greyhound and collie ancestery, has every prospect of whelping easily, I would never leave a bitch unattended when she is giving birth, particularly with a first litter: not that I am suggesting unwarranted interference but just a presence there to comfort and encourage her in her travail, and to ensure that contractions at frequent intervals result in the birth of a puppy before the bitch is exhausted.

The immediate forerunner of the first puppy is generally the appearance of a bladder-like bag and within an hour the first puppy will be born – often much sooner. It will be enclosed in the bag which is attached to the afterbirth (placenta) and umbilical cord. Most bitches instinctively bite open the bag and then chew through the cord to release the puppy, before licking it clean, but some maidens are flustered by this new experience until the first puppy is suckling and she realises what it's all about.

In her case some initial help is warranted. Anyone attending a birth must have scrubbed hands and finger-nails with the nails cut short – to guard against germs entering the bitch or the puppies while they are being handled. The first puppy can be released from its bag by the careful use of blunt-ended scissors; the cord is best severed about 5cm (2in) from the body by pinching it between the nails of the forefinger and thumb, using them in a grinding motion which simulates chewing – this method is better than cutting with an instrument, which can lead to minor bleeding. The puppy should lie in the nest while this is done, so that it is below the level of the afterbirth which, at this stage has not yet been expelled, because until moments before birth a reciprocal exchange of blood goes on between puppy and afterbirth, normally draining back to the puppy as it is born, but the opposite can occur if it is raised unnaturally at this time.

Once it is free, a finger can be used to clear the puppy's mouth and nostrils of any mucus, before it is guided to a teat. A strong one will begin to suckle within a minute or so. Meanwhile, the bitch resumes contractions to produce the afterbirth, which she will eat; this may seem revolting to humans but it is normal, providing her with protein and hormones to trigger milk production. When the first-born has been safely delivered and is sucking while the dam licks it, she can be allowed to take over, as it were, and cope with the remainder of the litter herself. She will appreciate a small drink of warm milk between births, but otherwise can be left to get on with her arduous job, while being watched for any sign of difficulty.

Deciding when to call a vet is often a difficult decision for a novice, but, as a general guide, prompt professional assistance is needed if the water bag has appeared (the first sign of imminent birth) and ruptured, and the bitch has been straining for more than an hour without result, then all is not well; the first puppy may be dead or in an attitude that makes birth impossible. Equally, if contractions have been steady but then cease, the bitch may be suffering from exhaustion or an inability to force a large puppy through her pelvic region. A vet may be able to manipulate it successfully or advise Caesarian section. Such problems are rare with lurchers, unless a pregnant bitch has been allowed to jump or play rough games with other dogs, or is in poor condition.

Granted normal births and a healthy litter, a bitch can be left to cosset her puppies and recover from the ordeal. After a much needed rest, the owner should inspect both the bitch and litter (speaking first to the bitch in congratulatory terms, because her protective instinct towards her litter will have developed by this time): the first thing to discover is whether or not she has sufficient functioning teats to feed the number of puppies; most have either eight or ten, but the pair nearest to the forelegs may be only vestigial and useless. This will mean that in a litter of eight or ten puppies two must be destroyed as they will not thrive; a grim decision but better than trying to rear two or more runts. Another good reason for limiting a litter is the age and size of the bitch: a large maiden lurcher bitch can rear up to eight puppies comfortably; a small one up to six; and without taxing their resources too much, assuming that they are given proper care.

The author with a pair of deerhound/greyhound X greyhound/wolfhound puppies. Although the greyhound influence has been doubled and the wolfhound reduced to a quarter the drop-ears persist and spoil the puppies as lurchers although they are examples of careful rearing and management.

Choosing the puppies to keep might be described as literally a choice between the quick and the dead: if there are several strong bitches these should be kept, because this is the most popular sex for sport; then, as puppies of all breeds are comparatively short faced (which means that the head is no guide), look for a long body presaging a greyhound outline; coat-length is difficult to assess in a new-born puppy but the suggestion of a wave in the hair indicates a lengthy rough coat. Any doomed puppies must not be removed while the dam is present, because this would upset her at a time when it is important for her to be calm and content; wait until one person can persuade her away to relieve herself in the garden and then sort the puppies, putting any rejects into a box to be taken away to the vet. At the same time, the bedding should be changed, replaced by a dry, warm piece of blanket, and, since it is important that the bitch should have no reason to mistrust her human attendants, the discarded puppies must be removed out of sight, sound and smell, so that she will return to find a clean bed and all well with her litter – she will not notice if it is depleted in some degree. Drowning is, unquestionably, a barbaric method of destroying puppies and any that have to die should be treated kindly, placed in a box with a blanket under and over them and taken to the vet who will give them humane oblivion.

Assuming that the litter was born overnight, the bitch will not need solid food for twenty-four hours afterwards because the protein content of the eaten afterbirths will sustain her during that time; but she will require plenty of liquid in the form of warm milk. On the second day she should be given light nourishing food in two main meals, plus milk, beaten-up raw eggs and meat broth: the amounts according to her size. The object is to sustain her and her milk supply for the puppies, while not over-taxing her digestion. During the suckling period of five to six weeks, the demands made by the puppies will reach a peak at about three weeks, and then dwindle as they begin to take solid foods and progress towards weaning.

Warmth can be a problem especially in bad weather: it is a question of not producing 'hot-house flowers' at one extreme and not risking hypothermia at the other. As a general rule, if the puppies are quiet and contented, dividing their time between suckling and sleeping, then no extra heat is needed. On the other hand, if the litter is noisy and restless, and the ears and feet of the bitch feel cold, then more warmth is an urgent necessity – although the latter case should not occur if they are managed with forethought by a sensible owner.

Heat must be supplied in a safe way. Paraffin heaters and electric fires are not safe; the best heater is a dull-emitter infra-red lamp of the type used for piglets, which should be suspended over or near the puppies' bed at a height *not less* than 60cm (2ft) above the head of the bitch when she is *standing* (infra-red heat is penetrating and can burn if used incorrectly).

Rearing the litter

Puppies open their eyes and begin to hear when they are between ten and fourteen days old (before then, they are dependent only on a sense of smell). At three weeks the milk teeth start to erupt and when these are through the gums, felt by a finger inserted into the mouth, the puppies are ready to take solid food. This is best given in the form of raw meat, scraped to remove indigestible sinews; each puppy being fed separately, by hand at first, with amounts varying from a level dessert-spoonful for a whippet type to a heaped table-spoonful for a deerhound-bred puppy – one feed is enough on the first day.

At this stage, the bitch should be kept away from her litter for at least half an hour after she has eaten her own meal, otherwise she may revert to the wild dog habit of regurgitating part-digested food for her puppies. This is the only way a wild dog has of weaning puppies but it is undesirable for a domestic dog to do this, since the food is not only unsuitable but deprives the bitch of her proper sustenance.

By the time the litter is five weeks old, they should be getting five meals a day and the bitch will be away from them for longer and longer periods. The feeds can be divided into two meat, one cereal and two milk meals: the meat may be minced or chopped; the best cereal is a baby food, such as Farex or rusks, made into a mush with warm milk or stock when the puppies begin to eat, and this can be changed to a puppy biscuit meal as they grow. The best milk is goats' milk if it can be obtained, but Channel Island cows' milk is adequate, and it should not be diluted – this comparative analysis shows why:

	water	proteins	fats	sugar
Cow	97.4	3.4	3.8	4.8
Goat	84.1	4.0	3.8	5.0
Bitch	66.3	8.6	14.8	2.9

Weaning is achieved by feeding the puppies before the bitch returns to them, so that they take less of her milk each time and her supply dries up naturally. During the time that she is feeding her litter there is a great demand on her resources, and she will only remain in good condition if she is fed properly, but when the puppies are at the totally weaned stage her feeding should be reduced to suppress further milk production – returning to her normal routine of one, or possibly two, meals a day.

10 Ailments and Accidents

THE lurcher is a hardy dog and, on the whole, less liable to disease than some pedigree breeds which have become prone to hereditary malformations and diseases, largely due to inbreeding for show points. Furthermore, it has the advantage of hybrid vigour when it is a crossbreed between purebred parents, as in the case of greyhound/sheepdog or greyhound/deerhound lurchers. Nevertheless, hereditary defects should be looked for and avoided. Of these the most likely are cryptorchidism and congenital cataract.

CRYPTORCHIDISM (OR MONORCHIDISM): These are terms used to describe a male dog in which only one testicle has descended into the scrotum. This is commonly seen in racing greyhounds and is no disadvantage to these dogs which are seldom kept beyond middle age, but a lurcher with the prospect of a long life may contract cancer at the site of the missing testicle as it gets older unless this is removed by surgical operation.

CONGENITAL CATARACT and PROGRESSIVE RETINAL ATROPHY: These are inherited diseases occasionally found in sheepdogs but this is unlikely with stock bred from dogs registered with the International Sheepdog Society. The first causes blindness in puppies and the second a gradual loss of vision in young adults, but since its eyes are vital to a working sheepdog none with this defect would be registered.

Virus diseases

Five major killer diseases affect dogs. These are canine distemper, hard-pad, virus hepatitis, leptospiral jaundice and canine parvovirus. The first four are prevented in at least ninety per cent of cases by a combined vaccine given in two inoculations about two weeks apart when a puppy has been finally weaned from its dam's milk for a period of a month. Since the introduction of these vaccines the incidence of such diseases has diminished to a remarkable extent, but outbreaks still occur to underline the importance of vaccination and subsequent booster doses at regular intervals according to the advice of a vet.

It is as well to be able to recognise the symptoms of virus diseases because prompt diagnosis can make the difference between life and death for an affected dog.

DISTEMPER and HARD-PAD: The symptoms are similar to those in human gastric flu: there is fever with a temperature of 40.5°C (105°F) or more; there is discharge from the eyes and nose, and diarrhoea. A characteristic musty smell is often present in the dog. Veterinary treatment and careful nursing can save a victim of distemper but, sadly, survivors of hard-pad may suffer brain damage which leaves them with incurable chorea (St Vitus' dance).

VIRUS HEPATITIS (RUBARTH'S DISEASE) and LEPTOSPIRAL JAUNDICE (STUTTGART DISEASE): They are often lumped together as 'the yellows' by old fashioned sportsmen because both show symptoms of jaundice in the later stages. The first sign is gastro-enteritis with a high fever; the dog looks and is very ill and in the case of hyperacute hepatitis may be alive one day and dead the next.

All these diseases are contagious, which means that they are picked up by dogs sniffing where infected dogs have been or where rats run – some fifty per cent of a given population of rats can be carriers of leptospirosis without apparent harm to themselves.

CANINE PARVOVIRUS: This hit the dog population of Britain towards the end of 1978 after having been known for a while longer in North America and Australia. Research indicated that it is an aberrant form of feline infectious enteritis and as such a new disease to which dogs are highly susceptible. It attacks dogs of all ages and serious outbreaks have wiped out whole litters of puppies. The symptoms are high fever, vomiting, and blood-stained diarrhoea. Parvovirus is contagious, transmitted from all the bodily secretions of an infected animal, and commonsense therefore suggests that it is wise to inoculate against this disease any lurcher that attends shows or coursing meetings where it will be in contact with a number of strange dogs.

Skin parasites and diseases

Fleas are the commonest skin parasite, with lice second; while ticks and harvest mites are picked up from pasture land during the summer. The first two can be eradicated by using an insecticidal powder or shampoo specifically made for animal treatment. *Never* use a product containing DDT as this is poisonous to all animals.

FLEAS: It is useful to know the life cycle of a flea in order to deal with an infestation. A female lays eggs either on the dog itself or in crevices in kennel woodwork, the folds off upholstery or under carpets; the eggs hatch after about a week into minute larvae, which in turn make cocoons containing pupa and these hatch out as small black fleas that turn brownish with age. The whole process can be completed within three weeks but in cold weather the creatures may remain dormant until the temperature rises above 10°C (50°F). Warm summer weather is the peak flea time but centrally-heated houses with fitted carpets make year-long havens for these insects.

Eradication involves breaking the cycle. The dog should be powdered or shampooed to kill the active parasites and then treated again about ten days later to remove the larvae which have hatched from eggs remaining in the coat. Meanwhile, the dog's bed and bedding should receive similar treatment and so should parts of the house which are likely to be harbouring larvae or cocoons.

Tapeworms can use fleas as intermediary hosts for their eggs and it is as well to dose the dog against these parasites at the same time.

LICE: An itchy dog which shows no sign of fleas may have lice which are more difficult to see in the coat. They appear greyish and are often clumped along the spine or on the chest, causing scabs of skin debris or angry spots. Two types may be found. The biting louse lives on the skin, while the sucking louse punctures it to absorb blood and plasma, and this means that the latter if it is present in large numbers can have a very debilitating effect, particularly on a young dog. Treatment is the same as for fleas, and lice can also play host to tapeworms.

TICKS: Ticks can attach themselves to dogs running over land grazed by sheep or rabbits (hedgehogs are also martyrs to ticks). Before it has fed on a dog's blood a tick resembles a small black crab, but once it has buried its head in the skin the creature bloats so that it looks like a grey pea. At this stage they can be removed individually but it is essential not to pull them off as the head may be left imbedded to fester and possibly create an abcess. A tick can be induced to release its hold with a drop of undiluted antiseptic, such as Dettol, but I use a lighted cigarette on top of the 'pea' (to insure against burning the dog) and then remove the creature with tweezers. It should be burned or flushed down a drain.

In parts of southern Europe and some other countries these parasites may carry *tick fever*. This serious disease is caused by an organism which invades the tick and is then injected into the dog it bites.

HARVEST MITES (CHIGGERS): These microscopic parasites are also picked up in the countryside, usually in late summer, and commonly attack between the toes to give rise to violent itching and reddening of the skin. Sometimes they enter the ears to create symptoms of 'canker' (*qv*). In either case they are best treated with a lotion on the advice of a vet.

MANGE: Mites are responsible for three forms of mange: *sarcoptic* (red mange), *follicular* (black mange), and *otodectic* (ear mange). Both red and ear mange are highly infectious and may be passed from dog to dog by physical contact or from kennel walls and bedding, but these forms respond well to modern treatment given under veterinary supervision. Black mange is less infectious but often proves difficult to cure – leaving a dog with patches sometimes described as 'elephant skin'.

Any dog which shows bald patches, either scaly or inflamed, should be examined at once by a vet, who may need to take skin scrapings for analysis under a microscope in order to discover whether the cause is one of the manges, or possibly ringworm or dry eczema which can appear similar in the early stages.

RINGWORM: This is not a parasite but a fungi. It is transmitted from dog to dog and also from buildings and woodwork which have been rubbed against by infected cattle up to six months previously. Prompt treatment is required and modern drugs will effect a cure within a short time, but meanwhile it is urgent to find the source of the infection and to keep the dog isolated. The first sign is a circular (hence 'ring') scaly patch which is intensely itchy, and if this is left untreated more patches will appear and spread to join up and leave large areas of bald encrusted skin on the miserable sufferer.

ECZEMA: Eruptions on the skin caused by eczema may be in one of two forms: wet eczema is seen as a moist patch surrounded by an area of greasy hair which falls away to enlarge the patch. It is both itchy and painful, and exterior treatment involves gently washing the part and then applying an antibiotic powder. Dry eczema is so easily confused with mange or ringworm that veterinary diagnosis is vital.

Eczema is not a skin disease as such but a symptom of internal disorders, often aggravated by hot, humid weather, and is usually traceable to an incorrect diet. A reduction in starch, an increase in animal protein, and the addition of vitamin B in the diet is often all that is needed to prevent a further outbreak.

BLANE (NETTLE RASH): Unless the cause is known to be due to insect bites or nettle stings, blane may appear on dogs subjected to sudden exercise in hot, humid weather or it may be due to a digestive upset. In severe cases the head and ears may puff up, but the common symptom is a few lumps and bumps on the back and flanks. Sponging with luke-warm water gives some relief and the dog may be given a pinch of baking soda (bicarbonate of soda) in a spoonful of cold water.

Worms

Two parasitic worms are of importance in dogs: the roundworm in puppies and the common tapeworm which is most likely to be found in adult dogs, particularly those which run where sheep or rabbits graze.

ROUNDWORMS (TOXOCARA CANIS): All puppies should be dosed against these worms as a matter of routine, because an infestation can stunt growth and cause general unthriftiness. The safe modern drug is Piperazine citrate, which is sold under various brand names in pill form or as a pleasant syrup liked by puppies which is easier to administer. It is important to follow the manufacturer's instructions based on the age and weight of the puppy.

TAPEWORMS: A dog can contract tapeworms by eating grass or sheep or rabbit droppings, ingesting eggs which develop into a worm which may reach a length of 1m (3ft) or more once it is established. Other sources are fleas and lice which act as intermediary hosts for these parasites. However, unlike treatment against roundworms, a dog should *not* be dosed against tapeworms unless it shows clear signs of infestation. A dog with tapeworms is thin along the spine in spite of a voracious appetite which often includes eating filth. Worm segments, resembling flat whitish rice grains, may be seen in the droppings or attached to hairs under the tail. In this case the specific drug is Dichlorophen which is sold under brand names and is safe and effective.

Apart from the common tapeworm, other species of this worm, and *hookworms* and *whipworms* may infest a dog. Broad-spectrum drugs, best obtained from a vet, will eliminate all these.

Internal ailments

A healthy dog may vomit occasionally or pass loose droppings because of some minor upset, so it is a matter of common sense to see if the symptoms persist beyond an isolated instance, because in that case prompt veterinary attention is vital since these symptoms may herald the onset of any one of a number of serious ills.

GASTRITIS: This is characterized by refusal of food; constant vomiting or attempts to vomit; the dog drinks thirstily only to bring up the liquid immediately. There is a danger of dehydration and exhaustion and a vet must be called without delay.

ENTERITIS: In this case there is persistent diarrhoea, usually accompanied by vomiting, as most forms of enteritis also involve the stomach – gastro-enteritis. Since this is caused by inflammation of the bowel lining, blood may be present in the vomit or droppings. In both cases bacteria are involved, although the initial cause may have been rubbish or filth eaten by a dog (or more often a puppy) infested with worms or suffering from a lack of vitamin B. But *do not* give worm medicine to an ill dog except under veterinary supervision.

CYSTITIS and BLADDER STONES: While these are separate ailments they have similar symptoms and so may be considered together. The dog repeatedly urinates or attempts to urinate, sometimes showing blood in the water. Cystitis is caused by germs or fungi in the bladder, often aggravated by a chill – which underlines the importance of drying a wet dog. Bladder stones are formed most commonly from phosphate, which is sometimes the result of over-dosing with a mineral supplement. Diagnosis is by means of X-ray and the only treatment is surgical removal.

Canker

Canker is an old-fashioned term still in common use as a description of a number of ear disorders. A dog that shows symptoms of earache by scratching and shaking its head should be examined by a vet, who can diagnose the trouble and prescribe suitable treatment. 'Canker' must not be neglected, because not only is it very painful to the animal but it may be the first signs of otodectic mange. Other causes are harvest mites; eczema; inflammation caused by damp; excess wax; or the presence of a foreign body such as a grass seed. *Never* probe the ear.

Anal glands

These glands are part of a dog's scent mechanism used for territorial marking in association with urine, and the glands in the hind feet which function when a dog kicks the ground after it has relieved itself. There are two anal glands, found inside the anus, which normally cover the droppings with a musky secretion as they are passed. Occasionally these glands become blocked and impacted, giving rise to a painful condition which either prevents the dog from evacuating its bowels or causes it to howl with pain when it attempts to do so. A sign, sometimes mistaken for worms, is when a dog skates its rear end along the ground, which it does because this ailment is intensely itchy in the early stages.

A vet will treat the trouble by squeezing out the impacted material but it is liable to recur at intervals unless there is some alteration in the diet, because in most cases the cause is that the droppings are too soft to stimulate the action of the glands. Roughage in the form of lightly cooked green vegetables, including the stems, and beef shin bones which can be ground (not splintered) by gnawing will go a long way towards preventing the recurrence of impaction.

Mammary tumours

Bitches are prone to these tumours in middle and old age. The first symptom is a pea-sized lump under or near a teat, which may grow into one large lump or proliferate into several small ones. Most of these tumours are more or less malignant but often are so slow growing that a dog may reach the end of her days before surgery would be necessary. However, even a small lump should be examined, and monitored at intervals, by a vet because if surgical removal becomes necessary this is a simple operation provided that the cancer has not been allowed to spread.

Poisoning

In this chemical age there are a number of deadly poisons easily available on the shelves of garden shops and hardware stores. Among the most dangerous are weedkillers containing paraquat, slug pellets, and warfarin rat bait; yet none of these products is marketed with sufficient warnings about their potentially lethal nature. Who reads the small print on a label? All these and strychnine laid in baits for vermin kill innumerable dogs every year. I have had one unforgettable experience of poisoning when a much loved beagle of mine returned home from an illicit lone hunting trip to die in dreadful paroxysms resulting from eating meat laced with strychnine – in spite of police inquiries the culprit was never found, which was perhaps just as well because otherwise I might have been on a charge of grievous bodily harm!

Dogs can pick up paraquat while eating weed grasses. There is no known antidote for human beings, let alone dogs. But from a dog's point of view slug pellets, rat poison and strychnine are more dangerous because they are given an attractive taste.

TREATMENT: A dog suspected of having eaten poison must be rushed to a vet's surgery while someone else telephones to give details so that an antidote may be prepared pending its arrival. If delay is unavoidable, perhaps because of a long car journey to the surgery, the dog should be given an emetic so that the contents of the stomach are vomited, thus reducing the amount of poison absorbed into the system. The best emetic is a lump of washing-soda about the size of a hazel nut given as a pill, but failing this a heaped teaspoonful of common salt diluted in a little warm water will act almost as well.

It is vital *not* to give milk or any other oily liquid if there is doubt as to whether the dog may have taken a phosphorous poison because this would accelerate its deadly effect.

TOAD POISONING: The common toad can secrete a mild venom if it is picked up by an inquisitive dog. This is seldom, if ever, fatal, but can produce some alarming symptoms. The dog vomits repeatedly and slavers ropy saliva, and may become briefly unconscious. Rinsing the mouth with a TCP solution can help; otherwise, quiet and warmth will do the rest.

SNAKE-BITE: Britain has only one poisonous snake, the adder or viper, which lives in woodland and on the moors. I have spent most of my life in a part of England where adders are common but none of my dogs has been bitten in spite of several encounters with these snakes. A bite is usually the result of an accident: a dog blundering about in undergrowth disturbs an adder which bites in defence. The gape of an adder's jaws is comparatively small, which means that its fangs can inject venom only into a limb on a dog or into a human hand.

A bitten dog suffers pain and swelling in the part, convulsions and collapse with a faint heart beat. Immediate first-aid involves a tourniquet above the bite to prevent the poison spreading; incising the site to promote bleeding and then packing the cut as deeply as possible with permanganate of potash crystals. The dog may be given a little strong coffee or brandy to encourage the heart, while it is kept as quiet and warm as possible until veterinary help is obtained as a matter of urgency.

The same treatment applies in America and other countries where venomous snakes are common. Anyone exercising a dog where dangerous snakes are known to abound would be wise to carry a small quantity of permanganate of potash crystals, a sharp knife and a length of material which can be used as a ligature in an emergency.

Ailments of a bitch and her litter

While giving birth and suckling a litter is a natural function and the average bitch benefits both physically and mentally from the experience, just occasionally things can go wrong and so she needs watching for any symptoms that suggest all is not well.

METRITIS (INFLAMMATION OF THE UTERUS): It is normal for a bitch to show a certain amount of discharge for a day or so after whelping but if the discharge is foetid and she appears unwell, off her food and feverish, and has little or no milk, then prompt veterinary attention is vital. The cause may be a dead foetus, a retained afterbirth or some internal injury.

ECLAMPSIA (MILK FEVER): A bitch feeding a large litter may suffer an attack of milk fever because her body is being drained of calcium due to high milk production coupled with a diet lacking nourishment and minerals.

The symptoms are frightening: the bitch staggers and then goes down in a fit, her legs outstretched and head thrown back, the body shivering violently. Prompt veterinary treatment is of the utmost importance, because without it a bitch can die after a succession of spasms culminating in heart failure. A vet will give an intravenous injection of calcium borogluconate solution, which, if there has been no delay, should produce almost immediate recovery, and he will then advise on necessary aftercare of the bitch and her puppies.

MASTITIS (INFLAMMATION OF THE TEAT): This may appear at any time during the suckling period. Usually the first sign is that the bitch will lie down to feed her litter and then get up almost immediately because they are causing her pain. Examination will show that one or more of the teats is hot and tender. If the trouble is not spotted early, she will become feverish and off her food, while the puppies wail their hunger. A vet will prescribe antibiotic treatment but the problem is that the drugs given to the bitch will be transmitted to her puppies via her milk which can result in a fading litter (*qv*). Vitamin B and other extra vitamins appear to offset this danger in some degree.

In most cases mastitis can be traced to a lack of hygiene: dirt can be injected into the teat by the claws of a suckling pup if the whelping bed and the area around it is not kept clean, or the bitch herself may go to feed them when her chest and belly has a spattering of mud from a farm or stable yard. Therefore, prevention is a matter of cleanliness and clipping the tips of the puppies claws to reduce scratching.

FADING LITTERS: The advent of parvovirus (*qv*) has meant that losses amongst new-born puppies has increased. Other reasons include canine herpes, hepatitis, a disparity in the parental blood groups, and hypothermia. The common symptom is a litter which fails to suckle and the puppies crawl about the nest uttering characteristic mewing cries until they weaken and die. Since puppies in this condition are certainly going to die anyway, it may be necessary for a vet to sacrifice one for post-mortem examination so that the cause can be identified, when there may be some hope of saving the rest. The sole blame for a case of hypothermia rests with the owner who has kept the bitch and her litter in cold, draughty quarters.

Accidents

The lurcher is prone to all the accidents that beset other members of the greyhound family, which is most liable to fractures of the legs and toes and to tears in the skin. Dislocations sometimes occur while a dog is twisting and turning during coursing. It must be realised that any crippling injury is not only painful but very frightening for an animal because primeval instinct tells it that loss of movement spells death in the wild, and so it is important to be both soothing and encouraging while the dog is being treated, giving it reassurance and a sense of security. I have found that the palm of a hand laid on a sick or injured dog's shoulders has a remarkable effect, somehow transmitting confidence – this is also effective with the majority of horses.

FRACTURES: A dog with a broken leg may be carried in the arms with the injured part supported to prevent movement, but a big lurcher will need some form of improvised stretcher such as a coat or blanket carried between two people while a third controls the dog, keeping it still and laid flat.

The vet will treat a fracture either by setting the bone within a plaster cast, or pinning or plating. A lurcher which has inherited the tender skin of a greyhound or whippet may react badly to a cast, the edges of which are liable to rub deep sores, and in that case it is better for the dog to undergo surgery so that the bone can be pinned or plated. Fractures in full-grown adult dogs ususally mend with little trouble but young dogs have the complication of growth to contend with, which means that a plate may have to be removed to allow for this and to avoid the problem of crooked growth. This is such a problem that I have regretfully come to the conclusion that it is often kinder in the long run to have a puppy under six months put down if it has suffered a serious fracture (greenstick fractures are another matter), but this is a question to discuss with a vet.

Broken toes are a common accident, usually caused by a swerve which puts a tremendous weight per square inch on the twisting foot of a dog running at thirty miles an hour or more. The toe is reasonably easily set and should knit within about three weeks if the dog is kept quiet meanwhile.

Breaking a toenail is miserably painful. This most often occurs on a hind toe, again in the course of running, and the nail is torn out at the root to leave a bloody stump of 'quick'. In this case a few drops of a non-stinging antiseptic, such as TCP, can be gently applied to keep the part clean until a new nail grows. If, however, the nail is merely cracked across and is still in place it is sometimes possible to set it with sealing-wax applied warm, not hot, but this needs care to be successful.

WOUNDS: Barbed-wire can cause tears in the skin of varying severity when a dog struggles between two strands (I have seen a whippet virtually 'un-zipped' down the spine while doing this). Small wounds of this kind should be swabbed with an antiseptic solution, TCP or Dettol, to remove possible bacteria and then left to heal. Larger gaping wounds will need suturing by a vet; in this case do not apply any medication. At one time it was often difficult to keep a wound of this type closed when the two edges were stitched flat and liable to pull apart, but nowadays the technique of roll-suturing in which the edges are rolled together and then over-sewn, gives excellent results with little, if any scarring.

Puncture wounds caused by the teeth of another dog, a rusty nail or whatever, need careful treatment because while a superficial injury should be encouraged to heal, it may be important to keep a puncture open if there is a risk that dirt has been injected: if the point of entry heals over too soon an abcess can develop underneath. For this reason a puncture should be examined by a vet who will probably prescribe antibiotic treatment.

HAEMORRHAGE: If blood is pulsing from a wounded limb it is vital to stop the flow as quickly as possible by means of a tourniquet, which can be improvised with a handkerchief tied in a loop and then twisted tight with the aid of a pencil or stick. This should be released momentarily at intervals and *must not* be kept tight for more than twenty minutes, as a longer period could result in serious damage to a limb deprived of its blood supply. On parts of the body where a tourniquet cannot be used, the only solution is to hold the lips of the wound together between finger and thumb until professional help arrives.

Some more or less minor wounds, particularly in a foot or ear, may bleed copiously, and in this case an ice cube wrapped in a clean cloth can be applied to encourage clotting but *do not* use ice if the dog is in shock and warmth is important.

BANDAGING: Unless a vet advises otherwise, most injuries are best left open to the air to heal, provided that the dog is kept in clean quarters. However, a cut in the foot or lower leg may have to be bandaged in order to prevent dirt entering the wound. Bandaging should always consist of three layers: a pad of lint or gauze against the wound, then a layer of cotton-wool, and lastly a crepe (elasticated) bandage which, by its elasticity, prevents bandaging too tightly. The end should be kept in place with sticking-plaster because a knot encourages the patient to chew. In order to keep the dressing clean while the dog is out of doors the foot can be covered by a plastic bag, also held with sticking-plaster, but this must be removed after each outing – prolonged exclusion of air by a covering of plastic would lead to sweating and damp inside the bag.

SPRAINS AND STRAINS: Twisting and turning while running at speed can pull muscles, tendons and ligaments in a lurcher, leaving the dog painfully lame or with a stiff neck or back; the part swells and a bruise may show in a thin-coated dog. The best cure is rest: the patient should be kept warm in a soft, comfortable bed and discouraged from any activity (except when the dog has to go out to relieve itself); a mild embrocation, such as Pettifer's green oils, can be used and pain-killing tablets may be obtained from a vet.

Once on the mend, the dog should be given slow exercise on a lead, bringing it back into condition by degrees.

General Information

NORMAL TEMPERATURE: 38.5°C (101.5°F). Use a blunt-ended clinical thermometer, greased with Vaseline, and insert in the rectum.

PULSE: The rate is between 70–100 per minute, but a normally erratic beat requires an expert to diagnose any fault except when the pulse is markedly weak or slow.

RESPIRATION: Normal rate 15–25 per minute.

TEETH: The milk teeth begin to erupt from the gums of a puppy when it is three weeks old and it has a complete set of twenty-eight when it is about six weeks old. These are replaced by forty-two permanent teeth from about four months onwards. Sometimes the canines ('eye' teeth) grow up beside the milk tooth version which fails to fall out as it should. In most instances the provision of beef bones and other safe chewy objects will put matters right.

The medicine chest

Most dog owners tend to collect a variety of ointments, powders and potions, some under brand names bought from pet stores and others supplied at one time or another by a vet. The latter should be clearly marked to indicate its purpose and dated, because some drugs such as penicillin have a short 'shelf life'. I keep animal medicines in screw-topped jars of the type used for instant coffee, clearly labelling the contents and its application so that it is readily to hand in a crisis.

Apart from a home medicine chest or cupboard, it is wise to keep a dog first-aid box in the car. This should contain the basic necessities for treating minor accidents.

FIRST AID BOX:
1   blunt-ended surgical scissors
1   packet lint or gauze
1   packet cotton wool
1   crêpe bandage
1   small bottle of a made-up solution of antiseptic such as TCP or Dettol (according to makers instructions – probably in a ratio of 5–1 with clean water)

1   tube antiseptic ointment such as Zemol or Bob Martin's 92. As a rule it is not a good idea to use ointments intended for human use because these may contain substances injurious to an animal which licks its wound.
1   puffer-pack of antibiotic powder (obtained from a vet).
1   knob of washing soda about the size of a hazel nut. Keep this in a small plastic bag for use as an emetic for a case of suspected poisoning.

While most people who have kept dogs over a number of years learn by experience to treat minor ailments and accidents with home remedies, and to act sensibly in more serious cases, there are a few dog owners who are foolish enough to fancy themselves as amateur vets: undertaking the suturing of wounds (without benefit of anaesthetic), setting fractures, and attempting sundry other treatments which are strictly the province of a trained professional. This can be not only disastrous but also cruel. The majority of dogs and lurchers in particular are stoic animals, prepared to withstand these fumbling attentions but they should not be asked to do so.

11 Shows and Showing

NOW THAT shows are being organised in almost every part of the British countryside a new owner of a lurcher can learn a lot by attending some of these events: watching judging in progress and seeing which types of dog win, besides enjoying races and working obedience classes, and, not least, meeting fellow enthusiasts. Most shows are held in conjunction with some other event, such as a country sports fair, which has the advantage of introducing the best of these dogs to a wide public who would otherwise hardly be aware of their existence.

There is no official standard for lurchers and winning depends on an individual judge's opinion, but most agree about the desirable features on which they base their decisions.

Conformation of a Lurcher

In basic terms a lurcher should look as if it is closely related to a greyhound or deerhound; intrinsically tough, yet graceful in outline and clearly capable of the speed needed to course and kill its quarry because that is its job. The details that combine to give good conformation are:

HEAD: Long with powerful jaws, wider between the ears than a greyhound.

EYES: Bold, intelligent and kind; in general a dark eye is preferred – a yellowish eye often betrays a wilful dog. Blue eyes are sometimes inherited from merle sheepdog ancestery and are acceptable.

NECK: This should be long and muscular; the top line running back into the withers, the under line shorter.

SHOULDER: The blade well laid back for speed, with the forelegs hanging straight – neither tied-in nor out-at-elbows.

CHEST: Deep with well-sprung ribs to give plenty of room for heart and lungs. The area of the brisket between the forelegs should measure a hand-span – the equine measure of 10cm (4in).

Supreme Champion Sandy with her owner Mrs Pamela Sykes at Lambourn Lurcher Show, 1980. The show began in a small way, organised by a few enthusiasts in the early 1970s but has since become a major annual event which attracts around seven hundred dogs entered in thirty classes.

BACK: Long, but not disproportionately so, and well muscled.

QUARTERS: Sloping; the thighs muscular for driving power.

STIFLE: Good angulation, showing muscular second thigh. As in a greyhound, the hocks are close to the ground.

FEET: A cat-foot; strong, round and neat. The dog should be 'on its toes', not flat footed.

BONE: While the whole skeleton is important, bone applies to the limbs in particular. Bones of the legs should be strong but not coarse; flat in the forelegs and well developed below the knee where weakness can lead to fractures.

SIZE: From the point of view of a show schedule lurchers are divided as those above and below 56cm (22in). A small dog of whippet size or less is at a disadvantage, and so is a big, rangy dog of 76cm (30in) or more.

COAT: The length of coat is immaterial, although schedules list separate classes for rough and smooth lurchers. Weather-proofing, however, is important and this should penalise a soft rough coat or a thin smooth coat.

TEMPERAMENT: The dog should be alert, taking an interest in all that is going on around it, and showing a kindly nature towards both humans and other dogs.

Supreme Champion Lucy, a greyhound/ deerhound X sheepdog, with her owner Mrs Rosemary Lloyd at Lambourn Show, 1981.

Show schedules

Shows including lurcher classes may be found advertised in the sporting and local press. These events normally start at about 10 a.m. and go on through the day, with a break for lunch, to end sometime in the late afternoon, depending on the number of entries. Schedules vary but the following list of classes may be expected:

Dogs over 56cm (22in)
1 Rough dog.
2 Rough bitch.
3 Smooth dog.
4 Smooth bitch.

Dogs under 56cm (22in)
5 Rough dog.
6 Rough bitch.
7 Smooth dog.
8 Smooth bitch.

Any size
9   Puppy under 12 months.
10 Brace (Pair).
11 Veteran (7 years and over).
12 Championship (winners of classes 1–8 automatically qualify)

Organisers of smaller shows may reserve the right to amalgamate certain classes if the entries are low, which can mean that dogs and bitches of the same size and type are judged in one class. On the other hand, what may be described as classic events, such as the Lambourn Lurcher Show which is held annually in Berkshire, attract an almost unbelievable number of dogs and it is not unusual for several hundred to compete on the day.

Apart from ring classes, schedules may include obedience, cross-country jumping, and racing after a dummy hare over a distance of some 220 metres (248 yards) – all of which are fun for the dogs and their owners, and for spectators who can find the finer points of ring judging wearisome after a time. Some shows are run on the lines of a three-day event for horses: that is, points are awarded for show classes, jumping and obedience and the dog which accumulates the highest number of points is the overall winner. The theory behind this system is that a winning dog must prove itself fit and trained for work, but the problem is that a dog jumping 'cold' over a gate (instead of being in hot pursuit of game) can suffer injury, which deters many owners from entering this type of event. Racing, too, has its problems: a major one being that some over-excited dogs tend to fight – which is why track greyhounds are fitted with muzzles.

Showing

While a lurcher show is not taken with the seriousness of a Kennel Club show, competitors should remember that all the honorary officials have given considerable time and effort to organising the event and have a right to expect competitors to be in the ring on time and to behave nicely when they get there. The same applies to their attitude to the judge and his or her stewards. There will still be plenty of time for talking with old friends and meeting new ones in and out of the beer tent.

Most shows take entries on the field before judging starts, each dog being given a number which is worn by the handler – a safety-pin is useful

Small lurcher Champion
Sam, Reserve to the
Supreme Champion,
with his owner Mr Roy
Cox at Lambourn Show,
1981.

for attaching it. When the class is called all the entries congregate in the
ring and are then asked to walk one behind the other round the perimeter
so that the judge, standing in the centre, can assess them as a whole: the
handlers set off on the right-hand with the dogs on the left to give the judge
a side view as they go round at a controlled springy walk. After one or more
circuits the entries are called into line and then each dog is examined
individually. It will be required to stand on some flat surface, which may
be an old door or a sheet of hardboard rough side up, so that poor feet are
not hidden in grass, and should be encouraged to stand four-square in a
natural attitude and not in the exaggerated stance of a hackney pony which
some handlers (probably emigrants from the pedigree world) try to
achieve. The judge will check its conformation by sight and hand and then
ask the handler to take it up and back in order to show its action. At this
stage a novice can go wrong, moving too fast and allowing the dog to cavort
on the end of its lead, making an impossible task for the judge who wants
to see it actively trotting away and back in a straight line, eager but
controlled. A characteristic of a trotting lurcher is the habit of holding the
head rather low and poked forward, and this should not be corrected by

A shooting-stick makes a good ringside seat on a long day at Lambourn Show. In 1981 an average of a hundred dogs were entered in each class to make a total of 1300 entries.

pulling up the lead as this is natural to many of these dogs and will be accepted as such by a judge.

When this part of the ordeal has been completed, the judge is likely to bring forward several dogs, compare these again with those remaining and finally weed out all but the winning first, second, third and reserve, which are announced by the steward who distributes rosettes, and cash prizes if these are included.

Judging is essentially a question of comparison and a good judge is constantly looking from one dog to another in the course of a class, and if a dog happens to be sitting down scratching itself while its owner chats with a neighbour, the chances are that it will be passed over in favour of another which is being kept on its toes ready for just such a passing glance to stop and reconsider its placing in the line. Everyone agrees that lurcher shows are primarily for fun but it would be foolish to suggest that an owner enters the ring without some hope of a prize, and taking a little extra trouble to present the dog at its best can make the difference between a rosette and a polite dismissal from the arena.

A subject of often heated discussion is the feasibility of registering

lurchers with some form of governing body. Two factions argue about this; one insists that it would spell ruin, while the other tentatively suggests that being able to trace parentage, at least to the extent of knowing the breeds involved, would enable breeders to plan suitable matings and effectively reduce the numbers of mongrel dogs which now masquerade as lurchers. Standing on the sidelines, I can appreciate both points of view.

People interested in the sporting ability of dogs have been justifiably appalled by the degeneration seen in several breeds of show terriers and gundogs and consequently mistrust any form of registration, but the real problem with these dogs was not the fact of being registered with a kennel club but that superficial scarring (a torn ear or whatever) excludes a dog from the show ring and reduces its value, and this means that exhibitors are chary of allowing a successful show dog to work. After a few generations such dogs lose a hitherto inborn desire to do the job for which they were originally bred – this is seen in 'Lassie' collies, now useless to a shepherd, and recently, in English springer spaniels, many of whom refuse to retrieve, and the list goes on to include the Sealyham terrier which was bred in the 1800s for otter hunting and is now so heavy and short legged as to be hard pressed to catch a mouse.

On the other side of the coin, a considerable number of pedigree

A view of some of the entries in the brace class at Lambourn, showing the platform on which dogs must stand to be examined by the judge who then can see good or bad feet not hidden by grass. The setting for the show is the beautiful racehorse training grounds owned by Mr Peter Walwyn at Seven Barrows on the Berkshire Downs; a prehistoric site including seven Bronze Age tumuli.

Races are often included in lurcher show schedules, with a dummy 'hare' as the quarry. This line-up shows quick-release coursing slips in use.

whippet breeders not only show their dogs but course and race them as well, thus maintaining the hunting instinct and true conformation of the breed. The International Sheepdog Society has controlled the breeding of working border collies since its stud book was opened in 1910, restricting registration to dogs which have proved themselves at trials and to their progeny; a lapse in registration for one generation means that their offspring become ineligible until again proved in a trial. This system has established the superb trial-bred collie of today. Another independent body which was organised in the 1970s is the Jack Russell Terrier Club: its purpose is to further the breeding of these terriers, eliminating those of marked mongrel extraction and setting a standard of a type suitable for working against foxes, which does not penalise scars in the show ring. Registration is on a two-tier system consisting of a foundation register for puppies and an advanced register for dogs over fifteen months old, which qualify only after being inspected and approved by a club official. A certificate awarded by a MFH or Master of otter (mink) hounds will be recorded in the register.

Considering these types of registration it is not beyond the realm of

Waiting for the off. An unconventional method of slipping but no doubt effective.

The Country Fair held in the grounds of Chatsworth, home of the Duke and Duchess of Devonshire, attracted a big entry in the lurcher section. The Supreme Champion is seen here with her owner Miss Judy Ruddy in 1981, against the backdrop of the magnificent house.

A demonstration at Chatsworth designed to show the general public how lurchers work. In spite of a long start, the dog is fast catching up with the dummy 'hare', which is not surprising since a good lurcher can travel at more than 30 mph. Country fairs are becoming increasingly popular summer events and are valuable as a means of introducing country life to people who otherwise have no knowledge of various sports beyond sometimes sensational press reports.

imagination to conceive some form of lurcher registration which might be beneficial, provided that hunting and killing game coupled with intelligence and speed remained of prime importance.

This may be a suitable point to sound a note of warning to owners of valued lurchers. Enthusiasts come from a wide strata of society and there are rogues about who will take any opportunity to steal a good-looking dog, which will vanish without trace. Dogs have been taken from locked cars at shows and friends of mine had their beloved, in-whelp bitch taken from their cottage garden – in spite of advertisements and extensive enquiries, including a friendly Romany grapevine, she has never been seen since. This is the same sort of theft suffered by horse owners whose animals are spirited away in the night. In both cases the owners are left distraught, always wondering what has become of the poor animal.

12 First Catch your Hare …

THE owner of a lurcher is likely to accumulate an *embarras de richesse* of rabbits, hares and even venison, and, moreover, many find this meat altogether too gamey for their taste, even though it represents good cheap food for a family. The fault often lies with the management of the carcass and with its cooking and so it seems worthwhile for me to offer some advice on the subject.

The first question is how long should a carcass be hung. Years ago game was hung until it 'fell off the hook', which in other words meant that it was virtually putrid, but nowadays most people keep it just long enough for the meat to become tender. Meat is tender until rigor mortis sets in (a freshly-killed rabbit can be eaten for supper the same evening but it will be as tough as old boots the next day), and so the real purpose of hanging game is to cover the rigor period until the flesh again softens. The time depends to some extent on the weather, being shorter when it is humid and longer in icey conditions, but on average hares and rabbits are fit to eat after two to four days and venison after a week. It is vital to keep blow-flies away meanwhile, which can be done by hanging in a fly-proof game larder or meat safe. Rabbits should be gutted soon after killing; hares are hung without gutting or paunching; and deer should be skinned and butchered before being hung.

Rabbit

Whatever the recipe, rabbit meat should be soaked in water overnight to bring out the blood; the strong flavour of adult wild rabbits can be reduced by adding a little salt and/or vinegar to the water. The meat is then patted dry with a clean cloth before being prepared.

ROAST RABBIT: Take a whole rabbit (minus its head which looks revolting in a dish) and wipe the body cavity dry before lining with bacon pieces and then filling it with sage and onion stuffing, which may need to be stitched in place with fine string and a trussing needle. It should be set underside down in a roasting dish with about a quarter of a pint of bitter beer or cider and cooked in a pre-heated medium oven for approximately an hour, basting at intervals. The liquid should be used as gravy, and the dish served with roast potatoes, onions or parsnips, a green vegetable and red current jelly.

CURRIED RABBIT: A rabbit must be jointed for this recipe: remove the hind legs at the hip joint; cut the body through the spine into two or three pieces, cutting the portion with the forelegs lengthwise. Fry some thinly sliced onions in butter until brown, then fry the rabbit pieces on both sides and transfer both to a saucepan with a curry sauce in half a pint of stock (which can be made by stewing the liver, heart and kidneys), and stew until the meat is tender. I cheat with this recipe, using canned mulligatawny soup to make the curry. Serve with rice, chutney, and a salad.

RABBIT PIE: Joint the rabbit and place in a pie dish with about half a pound of bacon pieces and some forcemeat balls (*qv*); three-quarter fill the dish with stock and cover with flaky pastry. Cook in a hot oven for ten minutes to set the pastry and then at a lower temperature until the meat is done. Serve with boiled potatoes and root and/or green vegetables.

CREAMED RABBIT: First boil the rabbit joints until tender with a few peppercorns and cloves, a chopped onion and a carrot. Then fry in a little fat an onion, about three celery stalks and two rashers of bacon, all chopped small; add three tablespoons of flour, stir it well in and add three quarters of a pint of the rabbit stock, slowly so as to make a smooth sauce. Remove the rabbit meat from the bones, chop it, and put it into the simmering sauce with salt and pepper and a tablespoon of lemon juice. Cook gently for ten minutes and serve in a border of mashed potato, liberally sprinkled with chopped parsley.

RABBIT BRAWN: Bring to the boil and then simmer one rabbit with some bacon pieces, an onion, a carrot and a small turnip, and add two teaspoons of salt and a *bouquet garni* consisting of a bay leaf and a sprig each of thyme and parsley. Strain the liquid, remove the meat from the bones and cut into cubes. Then dissolve two tablespoons of gelatine in half a pint of hot liquid and allow to cool until it is on the verge of setting before adding the meat and pouring into a mould or pudding basin. The brawn can be turned out when cold, sliced and served with salad, especially watercress.

Hare

The best way to cook a hare depends on its age. A young hare is termed a leveret until it is a year old and at this stage is tender enough to cook in several ways; it can be recognised by its short, sharp claws and soft ears, whereas an older hare has blunt claws, tough ears and a wide cleft in its lip.

Those who dislike the strong flavour should soak it overnight in the same way as a rabbit, with salt and vinegar added.

ROAST HARE: A leveret can be roasted in exactly the same way as a rabbit but for a longer time; beer or cider may be used or replaced by supermarket red plonk. Since both hare and rabbit tend to look unattractive when cooked whole, the dish needs adorning with plenty of vegetables and sprigs of parsley and watercress.

HARE PIE: Again only leverets are suitable for this recipe which is the same as rabbit pie.

JUGGED HARE: This is the traditional way to cook a hare, particularly older animals which are likely to be tough. Some years ago I inherited a set of recipes and household hints compiled by a forebear in the late 1700s and have extracted her recipe as an example of the original method. Incidentally, a jugg was a taller, narrower version of a modern glazed earthernware casserole.

'Cut the hare in pieces and put in a jugg, then set it in a kettle of water. Let it stew only in its own blood for three hours. Put in much salt as will lay on two shillings, a quarter of a pound of fat bacon cut small, half an onion, half a nutmeg, a dozen corns of black pepper, two sprigs of thyme, one of savory, two anchovies and a little red wine; let them stew all together. When you take it up put a quarter of a pound of butter and shake it together'.

I have tried, minus the butter, and found it strong meat but good on a cold winter evening if one has spent the day out in bitter weather. The lady quotes several recipes from her contemporary, Mrs Glass, who wrote the phrase 'First catch your hare ...' (which is so often wrongly attributed to Mrs Beeton), and also gives advice varying from how to remove wine stains from leather breeches to treating a large greyhound for worms with a mixture of powdered glass and lard.

A milder version of jugged hare involves frying the joints and placing them in a casserole with two sliced onions, six cloves, three whole allspice, half a teaspoon of pepper and two teaspoons of salt, a little lemon rind and a *bouquet garni*; then cover with a thick sauce made from two tablespoons of butter and three of flour mixed with a liquid consisting of half a pint of stock, quarter of a pint of vinegar and half a pint of cider, beer or red wine. It should be cooked slowly for three or four hours and served with forcemeat balls, red currant jelly, boiled potatoes and a green vegetable.

HARE SOUP: This can be made from the remnants of roast or jugged hare. Pick the meat from the bones and dice it; stew the bones with one large onion stuck with cloves, one sliced carrot, three celery sticks cut in short lengths and a trimmed slice of stale white bread, in about three pints of stock. Simmer until the vegetables are cooked; then remove the bones, add the meat and put through a blender (or failing that a sieve); thicken with flour and add a glass of port (or cheaper red wine), a tablespoon of red currant jelly and a squeeze of lemon juice. Boil up and serve.

FORCEMEAT: This can be used as a stuffing or formed into golf-ball sized balls and fried. The ingredients consist of six tablespoons each of breadcrumbs and suet, one tablespoon of chopped parsley, one teaspoon dried thyme or savory, half a teaspoon of salt, a pinch of mace and a generous one of pepper, a little lemon rind and an egg, to which is added the fried and chopped liver of a rabbit or hare. Use enough milk to bind the mixture.

GAME PATÉ: Either rabbits or hares or a mixture of the two can be made into an excellent paté which will keep for up to three weeks in a refrigerator. Remove the cooked meat from the bone and add it, including the liver and kidneys, to a mixture of two tablespoons of breadcrumbs, a large chopped onion, one egg, a few bacon pieces, half a teaspoon of salt, a good pinch of pepper, and pinches each of dried parsley, thyme, savory and mace (these amounts are for a total of 1kg (2lb) of meat and can be adjusted accordingly). Mix thoroughly, using a little melted bacon fat to bind if necessary, and then put through a blender or chop as finely as possible. Pack the mixture into a glazed earthenware jar and steam for two hours for 1kg and another fifteen minutes for each extra ½kg (1lb). Seal the jar with clarified butter or melted lard.

Venison

Since roe is the most likely species of deer to be caught by lurchers, I will use it as an example. A full-grown buck should kill-out at about the same weight as a lamb: that is, provide about 20kg (40lb) of edible meat on the bone plus offal. The carcass is butchered into haunches (leg and loin together), shoulders, cutlets and chops, and steaks cut from the loin. Those who dislike the flavour of venison can soak the meat overnight in salted water with a little vinegar added, and then steep it in warm milk and water for half an hour or so before cooking.

ROAST VENISON: The joints used for roasting are loin, leg (a whole haunch is too big for the average oven) and shoulder. The meat should be covered with thinly-sliced mutton fat or a smear of butter and a little red currant jelly, and cooked wrapped in foil in a pre-heated moderate oven, allowing 20 minutes per ½ kg (1lb); open the foil for the last half hour to allow the joint to brown. Serve with brown gravy, red currant jelly, roast potatoes and a green vegetable.

STEAKS, CUTLETS AND CHOPS: These should be cut not more than 2.54cm (1in) thick and are best grilled for about twenty minutes, turning every two minutes. Serve with a knob of parsley butter; mushrooms go well with grilled venison and so do jacket potatoes, and the ubiquitous red currant jelly.

VENISON CASSEROLE: Cut the meat in pieces and mix it with mushrooms and as many kinds of root vegetable as possible; season with salt, pepper and mixed herbs, and place in a casserole dish with enough stock to swamp it. Cook in a moderate oven for at least two hours. Serve with boiled or mashed potatoes. I have used canned turkey soup in this casserole and it was most successful.

Rabbits, hares and venison are not good subjects for freezing, losing much of their flavour in the process and often becoming tough as well.

Glossary of Terms

BABBLER: A dog which gives tongue when it should be mute.

BLAZE: White streak running up the face between the eyes. Usual in sheepdogs.

BONE: Strong but not coarse limbs.

BRINDLE: Dark and light hairs streaking a basically brown or grey coat.

BRISKET: The chest between and immediately behind the forelegs.

CAT-FEET: Neat round feet like those of a cat, desirable in all the greyhound family.

CHARACTER: Combining intelligence with correct conformation.

COUPLINGS: The body between the shoulders and hips – 'long-coupled' or 'short-coupled'.

COW-HOCKED: When, viewed from the rear, the hocks point inwards instead of being parallel and straight.

CROUP: Area of the back immediately in front of the root of the tail.

DAM: Female parent.

DEW-CLAWS: Supernumerary claws round on the front legs of all dogs and on the hind of some sheepdogs.

DROP-EARED: Pendant ears hanging close to the face.

EARTH: Foxes' lair.

FLY-EARED: Ears erect but falling forward at the tips. Common in collie-bred lurchers.

HARE-FEET: Long feet with separated toes. Undesirable in all greyhounds and lurchers.

HOCK: Joint on the hind leg below the stifle.

LEGGY: Disproportionately long legs.

MERLE: Coat bluish-grey, patched or streaked with black. Seen in collies, often in conjunction with blue eyes.

OESTRUS: Time during which a bitch will mate. Spelt *estrus* in North America.

OUT-AT-ELBOWS: Instead of hanging straight from the shoulder, elbows point outwards.

OVER-SHOT: Upper jaw projects so that the teeth do not close correctly.

ROACH-BACK: Desirable in moderation for whippet and Italian greyhounds, when the loins are arched.

ROSE-EARED: Drop ears folded over and back to reveal interior, seen in most greyhound breeds and inherited by lurchers.

SELF-MARKED: A dog of a single colour with white on the chest, feet and tail tip.

SEASON: Term for oestrus period.

SHELLY: A thin, badly-constructed dog.

SIRE: Male parent.

SPLAY-FEET: Toes are widely spread. Most undesirable in coursing dogs.

STIFLE: First joing below the hip.

TUCKED-UP: This terms can be confusing as it has two meanings: one describes the greyhound type, deep-chested with the loins arched to give a racey appearance; the other is a derogatory description of a sickly dog with it flanks drawn in.

UPRIGHT SHOULDERS: The shoulder blade is too straight instead of being set at a slight angle for speed.

VARIETY MEATS: Term used for offal in North America.

VIXEN: Female fox.

WALL-EYED: Blue eyes, common in merle sheepdogs and sometimes transmitted to their lurcher progeny.

WHELPING: The birth of puppies.

Appendix 1: Further Reading

Arrian, Flavius	*On Coursing* (AD150)★
Berners, Julyana	*Ye Boke of Huntying* (circa 1400)★
Blaine, Delabeare P.	*Encyclopaedia of Rural Sports* (1840)★
Cousens, F.W.	*Dogs & Their Management* (1946)★
Drabble, Phil	*Of Pedigree Unknown: Sporting and Working Dogs* (Michael Joseph, 1976)
Edwardes-Clarke, H.	*Waterloo Cup* (Saiga, 1978)
Foix, Gaston de	*Le Livre de Chasse* (1390)★
Plummer, David Brian	*The Complete Lurcher* (Boydell Press, 1979)
	Lambourn (Boydell Press, 1980)
Taplin, William	*The Gentleman's Cabinet* (1803)★
Twici, Guillaume	*Treatise on Hunting* (circa 1350)★
Vesey-Fitzgerald, B.	*Book of the Dog* (1946)★
Walsh, Col E.G.	*Lurchers & Long-Dogs* (Standfast Press, 1978)
Wood, Rev .J.G.	*Illustrated Natural History* (1874)★
Xenophon	*On Coursing Hounds* (circa 350 BC)★

★Out of print

Appendix 2: Useful Addresses

Great Britain

Animal Health Trust, 24 Portland Place, London W1N 4HN
British Field Sports Society, 59 Kennington Road, London SE1
Country Gentlemen's Association, Icknield Way West, Letchworth, Herts. SG6 4AP
The Dogs Home, 4 Battersea Park Road, London SW8 4AA
The Field, Carmelite House, London EC4Y OJA
Lambourn Lurcher Show (Honorary Secretary), Westcot House, Westcot, Wantage, Oxon OX12 9QA
Retired Greyhound Trust, 140 Tottenham Court Road, London, W1P 0AS
Shooting Times, 10 Sheet Street, Windsor, Berkshire SL4 1BG

USA

American Kennel Club, 51 Madison Avenue, New York, NY 10010
Field and Stream, 1515 Broadway, New York, NY 10036

Australia

Australian Outdoors, 142 Clarence Street, Sydney, NSW 2000
South Australian Canine Association, Inc., Showgrounds, Wayville, South Australia 5034

NB A number of specialist breed societies operate rescue services for unwanted or ill-treated dogs, finding guaranteed kind, permanent homes. Addresses of such breed clubs can be obtained from The Kennel Club, 1 Clarges Street, Piccadilly, London W1Y 8AB.

Index